This book
...s to

© J. Sharples

TATTING PATTERNS

TATTING PATTERNS

Mary Konior

B. T. Batsford Ltd, London

Sugar and Spice with an antique ivory shuttle

Acknowledgment

With special thanks to Catherine Pickering and Teresa Withycombe, my daughters, for assistance in test-working the directions; to Carol Carsten and Gill Fisher, of the Ring of Tatters, for allowing me to include their designs; to Diana Cooper and family, for allowing me to include a design by Christine Appleton (deceased), also of the Ring of Tatters; to The English Lace School for allowing me to photo-graph tatting from their collection; to Wm Briggs & Co. Ltd, for permission to reproduce patterns from *Penelope Book 3*; and to J. & P. Coats (UK) Ltd, for permission to reproduce a pattern from *Learn Tatting, Book 660*.

ISBN 0 8521 9800 0

Typeset in Optima by Latimer Trend & Co. Ltd.
and printed in Great Britain by
Courier International, Tiptree, Essex

for the Publishers
B. T. Batsford Ltd.
4 Fitzhardinge Street
London WIH 0AH

A CIP record for this book is available from the
British Library.

CONTENTS

INTRODUCTION

Patterns new, patterns old,
Patterns borrowed, patterns cajoled

Lacemakers love to collect patterns, so no justification is needed for another pattern book: there will never be too many.

Here, therefore, is a collection of patterns for shuttle-lace, more generally known as tatting. It is based mainly on new work of my own but, in order to ensure a wide appeal to all tastes, I have gleaned ideas from several modern designers and from past traditions, giving full acknowledgment of the source where appropriate. Many classics have so proved their worth that they deserve to be re-presented with a fresh text, and introduced to tatters new to the craft. In addition, I have included some examples of roll tatting, pearl tatting and other multi-thread techniques, which are not well known and, I think, merit wider usage.

For each pattern there are detailed written instructions, with a clear photograph carefully chosen to act as a visual back-up to the text, so making any explanatory diagram(s) superfluous. The size and make of thread are given solely as a guide to measurements; there is no reason why either should not be changed at the worker's discretion. Raw beginners, especially, may prefer to use thicker threads than specified.

Patterns suitable for beginners are marked with a dagger †. It would seem logical to grade the remainder in order of difficulty, but I have avoided this because, once past the initial learning stage, different tatters will not necessarily develop new skills in the same sequence. That which one person would consider 'challenging', another would con-

sider 'average', and vice versa. For those who feel in need of a refresher course in the various techniques, a list of relevant books is given.

The beguiling structure of tatting has lured many devotees to try designing for themselves. My own strategem is to cut up discarded tatting and re-arrange the fragments, like pieces in a jig-saw puzzle. When a new arrangement seems promising, it is pinned to a suitable surface for safe keeping. The new design is then test-worked and amended as necessary. All this pre-supposes having an adequate assortment of pieces before one starts, and results in a mutilated litter of cuttings when one has finished. Even experienced tatters have been known to turn pale at these revelations, but the method is one which works for me. It is a very direct approach to creative design, and gives more realistic results than indirect planning with the aid of diagrams.

I use the term 'creative' with some misgiving. Although it has a well-understood meaning among craft workers, it has also become a vastly over-used epithet which, like house agents' jargon, has acquired negative undertones. It *can* be a synonym for 'results-haven't-quite-matched-expectations', or, 'there-aren't-going-to-be-any-instructions'. Happily, neither applies to this book.

Because thread is of paramount importance, manually, to any lacemaker, it is sometimes difficult to realise that visually, and paradoxically, its absence is as important as its presence. In constructing a design, the *negative* open spaces are of as much aesthetic value as the *positive* solid structures of the actual thread. Success depends on a good *gestalt,* that is, on a well-balanced arrangement of positive and negative shapes.

Although, theoretically, there may be no limit to the permutation of positive and negative shapes in tatting, there are some practical limitations. The overall structure has to hold together sufficiently to form a stable fabric—unless, of course, it is intended for appliqué, in which case the tatting should be classed as embroidery rather than as lace. There is also a limit to the number of times it is reasonable to finish ends and begin again in an individual piece of work—a point not recognised as important in many Victorian patterns, but of some consequence nowadays.

There are a number of stylised floral designs in this collection. Any resemblance to flower or leaf shapes in tatting is a natural phenomenon resulting from its basic structure, rather than from an intentional aim on my part, although I exploit this aspect shamelessly when naming a design. The names are, of course, an indulgence, purely for convenience in distinguishing one pattern from another, and therefore should have no great significance attributed to them. I hope I have avoided any horticultural anomaly, such as bestowing the name of a six-petalled flower on a five-petalled tatted formation!

Here, then, are the patterns. They cover a wide range of ventures, from the blatantly-ambitious major *oeuvre* to the only-slightly-breathtaking minor fragment. But even a tiny fragment need not be despised. It can be a convenient means for using waste thread, and can be enjoyed, virtuously yet frivolously, as the tatted equivalent of the toy in a cornflake packet.

READING THE INSTRUCTIONS

ABBREVIATIONS

ds — double stitch(es)
hs — half stitch(es)
rs — roll stitch(es)
Jk — Josephine knot(s)
p — picot(s)
rw — reverse work

Letters of the alphabet are used to identify particular rings and chains to clarify meaning whenever necessary.

The presence of a chain infers the use of both shuttle and ball threads. Where more than one shuttle or more than one ball is required, this is stated.

Quantities are given only where a specific finished article requires more than one 20g ball of cotton.

All photographs have been chosen for clarity of illustration, and should be sufficiently explanatory in the event of there being any ambiguity in the written directions.

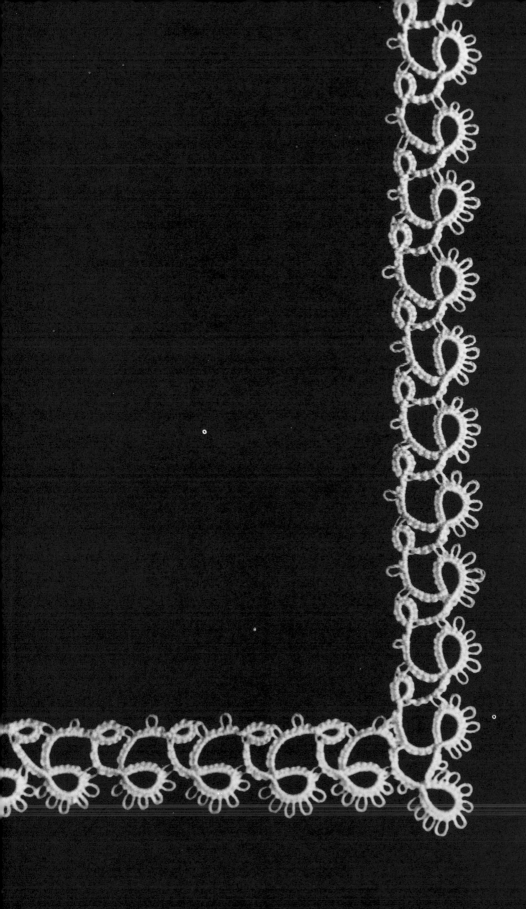

THE PATTERNS
Edgings with corners

CAMOMILE

Using Coats *Chain* Mercer Crochet No. 60, the edging measures 1.25 cm ($\frac{1}{2}$ in) in width.

Ring A of 7ds, p, (2ds, p) 5 times, 2ds.
Chain A of 3ds, p, 3ds, rw.
Ring B of 7ds, p, 7ds.
* Chain B of (3ds, p) twice, 5ds, rw.
Ring A of 7ds, join to Chain A, (2ds, p) 5 times, 2ds.
Chain A as before.
Ring B of 7ds, join to last picot of Chain B, 7ds.

Repeat from * for the length required, ending with Chain A for the corner. Do not reverse work.

Corner

Ring C of (2ds, p) 9 times, 2ds.
Chain C of (3ds, p) twice, 3ds, join shuttle thread to last picot of previous Chain B, rw.
Chain B as before.
Ring A of 7ds, join to last picot of previous Chain C, (2ds, p) 5 times, 2ds.
Chain A as before.
Ring B of 7ds, join to last picot of Chain B, 7ds.

Continue from * as before.

CELANDINE

Using Coats *Chain* Mercer Crochet No. 60, the edging measures 2 cm ($\frac{3}{4}$ in) at its widest and will adapt to a curve.

Corner flower

Ring of 7ds, p, (5ds, p) twice, 7ds.
* Ring of 7ds, join to last picot of previous ring, (5ds, p) twice, 7ds.
Repeat from * 4 times more.
Ring of 7ds, join to last picot of previous ring, 5ds, p, 5ds, join to first picot of first ring, 7ds.
Tie ends and finish.
Work three more corner flowers, or the number required, before commencing the leaf edging.

Leaf edging

Ring A of (5ds, p) three times, 5ds.
Ring B as Ring A.
Ring C of 5ds, join to last picot of previous ring, 5ds, join to any junction of rings on first flower, 5ds, p, 5ds, rw.
Chain A of 5ds, join to first picot of leaf Ring A, 5ds, p, 10ds, join shuttle thread to next junction of rings on flower, rw.
Chain B of 7ds, p, 5ds, p, 7ds, rw.
Ring D of 10ds, join to picot of Chain A, 5ds, p, 5ds.
Ring E of 5ds, join to previous ring, 5ds, join to centre picot of leaf Ring A, 5ds, p, 5ds.
Ring F of 5ds, join to previous ring, 5ds, p, 10ds, rw.

* Chain C of 7ds, p, 5ds, p, 7ds, rw.
Ring G of 10ds, join to last picot of previous ring, 5ds, p, 5ds.
Ring H of (5ds, p) twice, 10ds, rw.

Repeat from * for the length required, ending with Chain C in readiness for the next corner.

Ring I as Ring G.
Ring J of 5ds, join to previous ring, (5ds, p) twice, 5ds.
Ring K as Ring F.

Chain D of 7ds, p, 5ds, p, 7ds, join to any junction of rings on next flower, rw.
Chain E of 10ds, join to Ring K, 5ds, p, 5ds.
Ring L of 5ds, join to picot of Chain E, 5ds, join to centre picot of Ring J, 5ds, p, 5ds.
Ring M as Ring A.
Ring N of 5ds, join to last picot of previous ring, 5ds, join to next junction of rings on same flower, 10ds.
Tie ends and finish.

Repeat the leaf edging, joining to the relevant flowers as shown.

CROCUS

Using Coats *Chain* Mercer Crochet No. 20, the edging measures 2 cm ($\frac{3}{4}$ in) in width, and is an example of Roll Tatting.

Ring A of 4ds, p, 2ds, p, 6ds, rw.
* Chain A of (6ds, p) twice, 4ds, rw.
Ring B of 6ds, join to last picot of previous ring, 1ds, 30rs, 1ds, p, 6ds.
Ring C of 6ds, join to previous ring, 1ds, 12rs, 1ds, p, 6ds.
Ring D of 6ds, join to previous ring, 1ds, 30rs, 1ds, p, 6ds, rw.
Chain B of 4ds, join to last picot of previous chain,

6ds, p, 6ds, rw.
Ring E of 6ds, join to previous ring, 2ds, p, 4ds.
Ring A of 4ds, join to previous ring, 2ds, p, 6ds, rw.

Repeat from * for the length required, ending with Ring D for the corner. Do not reverse work.

Corner
Repeat Rings C and D once more.
Chain B of 4ds, join to last picot of previous chain, 6ds, join to next picot of same chain, 6ds, rw.
Continue from Ring E as before.

Using Coats *Chain* Mercer Crochet No. 40, the edging measures 2.5 cm (1 in) and will adapt to a curve.

Ring A of (3ds, p) twice, 6ds, rw.
* Chain of 9ds, p, 9ds, rw.
Ring B of 9ds, join to last picot of previous ring, 6ds.
Ring C of 6ds, join to junction of Rings A and B, (5ds, p) twice, 9ds.
Ring D of 9ds, join to last picot of previous ring, (6ds, p) twice, 9ds.
Ring E as Ring D.
Ring F of 9ds, join to last picot of previous ring, (5ds, p) twice, 6ds.
Ring G of 6ds, join to last picot of previous ring, 9ds, rw.
Chain as before.
Ring H of 6ds, join to junction of Rings F and G, 3ds, p, 3ds.

Ring I of 3ds, join to previous ring, (4ds, p) twice, 6ds, rw.
Chain as before.
Ring J of 6ds, join to last picot of previous ring, (4ds, p) twice, 3ds.
Ring A of 3ds, join to last picot of previous ring, 3ds, p, 6ds, rw.

Repeat from * for the length required, ending with Ring A for the corner.

Corner
Chain as before.
Rings B, C and D as before.
Repeat Ring D three times more.
Rings F and G as before.
Chain of 9ds, join to previous chain, 9ds, rw.
Continue from Ring H as before.

HEDGEHOGS

This is a classic single-thread edging, as illustrated in Lady Katharin Hoare's *Art of Tatting* (1910). Using Coats *Chain* Mercer Crochet No. 40, the edging measures 2.25 cm ($\frac{7}{8}$ in) in width.

Ring A of (2ds, p) 10 times, 2ds. Space of 3 mm ($\frac{1}{8}$ in).
Ring B of 4ds, join to nearest picot of Ring A, 4ds, rw. Space as before.
Ring C of 3ds, p, (2ds, p) four times, 3ds, rw. Space as before.
Ring B of 4ds, join to next picot of Ring A, 4ds, rw. Space as before.
* Ring C of 3ds, join to last picot of previous Ring C, (2ds, p) four times, 3ds, rw. Space as before.
Ring B as before.

Repeat from * five times more. Take the thread to back of work and tie to centre picot of last Ring C. Leave a space of 1.25 cm ($\frac{1}{2}$ in).
Ring A and first Ring B as before.
Ring C of 3ds, (p, 2ds), twice, join to picot where thread is tied on previous group, (2ds, p) twice, 3ds, rw. Space as before.
Complete the 'hedgehog' as before, and repeat as required.

Corner
Work a corner Ring A of 11 picots instead of the usual 10, and repeat Rings B and C around the entire corner ring as shown.

Using Coats *Chain* Mercer Crochet No. 20, the edging measures 3.5 cm (1¼ in) in width. Two shuttles are needed for the second row.

First row

Ring A of 6ds, p, 4ds, p, 8ds, rw.
* Chain A of 9ds, p, 2ds, p, 7ds, p, 9ds, rw.
Ring B of 8ds, join to last picot of Ring A, 4ds, p, 6ds.
Ring C of 7ds, p, 7ds.
Chain B of 4ds, p, 4ds, rw.
Ring D of 4ds, join to last picot of Chain A, (2ds, p) twice, 4ds, rw.
Chain C of 4ds, p, 4ds.
Ring E as Ring C.
Ring F as Ring A.
Chain D of 9ds, join to last picot of Ring D, 7ds, p, 2ds, p, 9ds, rw.
Ring G of 8ds, join to last picot of Ring F, 4ds, p, 6ds.
Ring A of 6ds, join to last picot of Ring G, 4ds, p, 6ds, rw.

Repeat from * for the length required, ending with Ring E for the corner.

Corner

Ring C, Chain B as before.
Ring D of 4ds, join to last picot of previous Ring D, 2ds, join to next picot of same ring, 2ds, p, 4ds, rw. Continue from Chain C as before.

Second row

Using two shuttles wound on a continuous thread, join to free picot of first Ring B. Use the main shuttle as working shuttle for the chains, and use the second shuttle for the Josephine knots.
* Chain A of 4ds, Jk of 10hs, continue chain with 4ds, join main shuttle thread to next Ring C.
Chain B of (4ds, Jk) three times, 4ds, join main shuttle thread to next Ring E.
Chain C of 4ds, Jk, 4ds, join main shuttle thread to next Ring F.
Chain D of (4ds, Jk) twice, 4ds, join main shuttle thread to next Ring B.

Repeat from * all around, omitting Chains C and A at the corner as shown.

PUNCH AND JUDY† _____

Using Coats *Chain* Mercer Crochet No. 40, the edging measures 2 cm (¾ in) in width.

Ring A of 6ds, p, (3ds, p) twice, 6ds.
Ring B of 6ds, join to last picot of previous ring, (1ds, p) six times, 6ds.
Ring C of 6ds, join to last picot of previous ring, (3ds, p) twice, 6ds, rw.
Ring D of 6ds, p, (3ds, p) twice, 6ds.
* Ring E of 6ds, join to last picot of previous ring, 3ds, p, 3ds, large p, 6ds, rw.
Ring A of 6ds, join to last picot of Ring C, 3ds, join to next picot of same ring, 3ds, p, 6ds.

Rings B and C as before.
Ring D of 6ds, join to large picot of Ring E, (3ds, p) twice, 6ds.

Repeat from * for the length required, ending with Ring C for the corner. Do not reverse work.

Corner

Work Rings B and C once more.
Ring D of 6ds, join to large picot of previous Ring E, 3ds, join to centre picot of same ring, 3ds, p, 6ds.
Continue from Ring E as before.

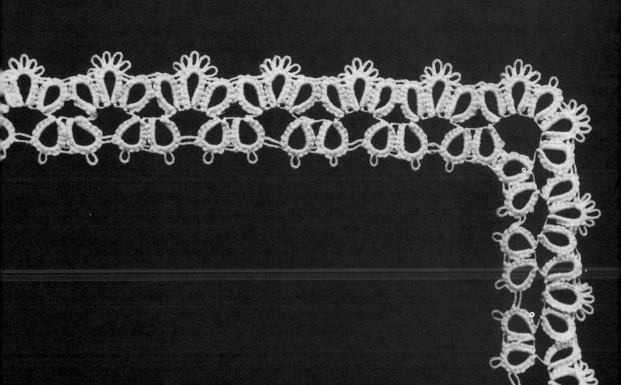

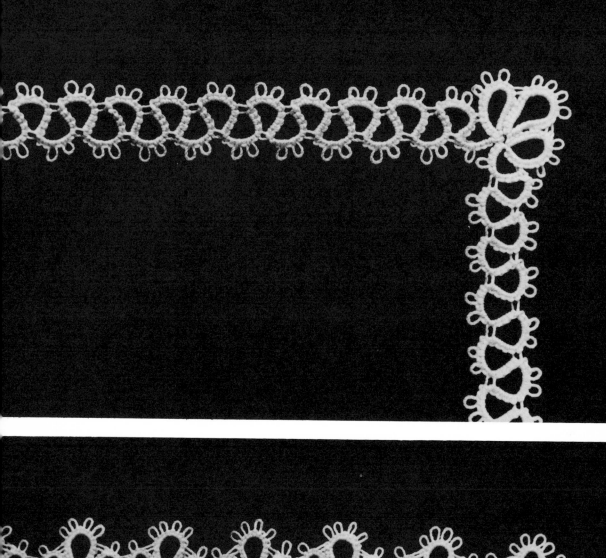

SNAKE CHAIN

The continuous snake chain has been a classic since the 1920s. Many tatters appreciate the fact that the shuttle seldom needs refilling with this pattern. Using Coats *Chain* Mercer Crochet No. 60, the edging measures 1.25 cm ($\frac{1}{2}$ in) in width and will adapt to a curve.

Start at the corner:
Ring A of (4ds, p) twice, (2ds, p) three times, 8ds.
Ring B of 8ds, join to last picot of previous ring, (2ds, p) five times, 8ds.
Ring C of 8ds, join to last picot of previous ring, (2ds, p) three times, 4ds, p, 4ds, rw.

Snake Chain

Chain A of 4ds, p, 2ds, p, 4ds, join shuttle thread to last picot of Ring C, rw.
* Chain B of (2ds, p) three times, 4ds, join shuttle thread to last picot of previous chain, rw.

Repeat from * for the length required to reach the next corner, ending at the inner edge.

Chain C of 2ds, p, 4ds, rw.
Ring A of 4ds, join to last picot of previous Chain B, 4ds, p, (2ds, p) three times, 8ds.
Continue from Ring B as before.

SUGAR AND SPICE

Using Coats *Chain* Mercer Crochet No. 40, the edging measures 2.5 cm (1 in) in width.

Ring A of 5ds, p, (3ds, p) twice, 5ds.
Ring B of 5ds, join to last picot of previous ring, 5ds, p, 5ds, rw.
Ring C of (5ds, p) twice, 5ds.
Ring D of 5ds, join to last picot of previous ring, (2ds, p) three times, 7ds.
* Ring E of 7ds, join to last picot of previous ring, (2ds, p) five times, 7ds.
Ring F of 7ds, join to last picot of previous ring, (2ds, p) three times, 5ds.
Ring G of 5ds, join to last picot of previous ring, 5ds, p, 5ds, rw.
Ring H of 5ds, join to Ring B, 5ds, p, 5ds.
Ring I of 5ds, join to previous ring, (3ds, p) twice, 5ds.
Ring A of 5ds, join to last picot of previous ring, (3ds, p) twice, 5ds.
Ring B as before.
Ring C of 5ds, join to Ring G, 5ds, p, 5ds.
Ring D of 5ds, join to previous ring, 2ds, join to corresponding picot of Ring F, (2ds, p) twice, 7ds.

Repeat from * for the length required, ending with Ring E for the corner.

Corner
Corner ring of 7ds, join to last picot of previous ring, (2ds, p) three times, 7ds.
Repeat corner ring once more.
Rings E, F, G and H as before.
Ring I of 5ds, join to previous ring, 3ds, join to centre picot of Ring A, 3ds, p, 5ds.

Continue from Ring A as before.

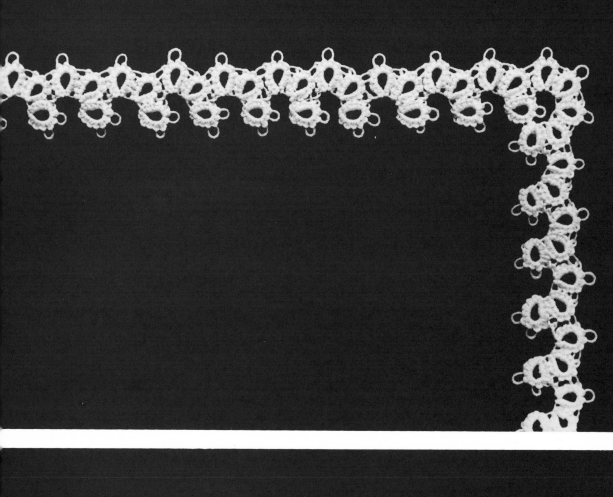

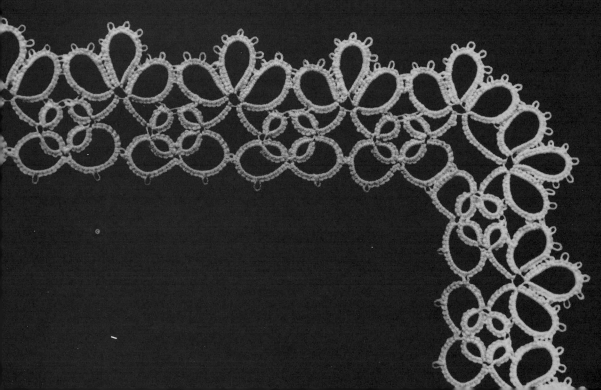

THREE BLIND MICE†

Using Coats *Chain* Mercer Crochet No. 40, the edging measures 1.5 cm ($\frac{5}{8}$ in) in width and will adapt to a curve.

Ring A of 4ds, p, (2ds, p) twice, 4ds.
* Ring B of 4ds, join to last picot of previous ring, (2ds, p) twice, 4ds.
Ring C as Ring B.
Take shuttle thread to back of work and join it to the junction of Rings B and C.
Ring A of 4ds, join to centre picot of Ring B, (2ds, p) twice, 4ds.

Three Blind Mice

Continue from * for the length required, ending with Ring C for the corner.

Corner

Rings D and E as Ring C (thus making a corner group of five rings).
Join shuttle thread to last picot of previous group of three rings, then take the thread to back of work and join it to the junction of Rings D and E.
Ring A of 4ds, join to centre picot of Ring D, (2ds, p) twice, 4ds.

Continue from Ring B as before.

VICTORIAN TREFOIL EDGING

A prototype of this design appeared in *Weldon's Practical Tatting* in 1889, and it has remained popular ever since. Examples can sometimes be found on underwear of the period. Using Coats *Chain* Mercer Crochet No. 20, the edging measures 4 cm ($1\frac{1}{2}$ in) in width.

Ring A of 5ds, p, 2ds, p, 7ds.
Ring B of 7ds, p, 7ds, rw.
Chain A of (7ds, p) twice, 7ds, join shuttle thread to Ring B, (7ds, p) twice, 7ds, rw.
Ring C of 7ds, join to junction of Ring B and Chain A, 7ds.
Ring D of 7ds, join to corresponding picot of Ring A, 2ds, p, 5ds, rw.
Chain B of 7ds, rw.
Ring E of 7ds, join to Ring D, 7ds, p, (3ds, p) four times, 7ds.
* Ring F of 7ds, join to last picot of previous ring, (3ds, p) six times, 7ds.
Ring G of 7ds, join to last picot of previous ring, (3ds, p) four times, 7ds, p, 7ds, rw.
Chain C as Chain B.
Ring A of 5ds, join to last picot of previous ring, 2ds,

p, 7ds.
Ring B as before.
Chain A of 7ds, join to last picot of previous Chain A, 7ds, p, 7ds, join shuttle thread to Ring B, (7ds, p) twice, 7ds, rw.
Rings C, D and Chain B as before.
Ring E of 7ds, join to Ring D, 7ds, join to corresponding picot of Ring G, 3ds, join to next picot of same ring, (3ds, p) three times, 7ds.

Repeat from * for the length required, ending with Ring G for the corner.

Corner

Chain of 13ds, rw.
Ring E of 7ds, join to last picot of Ring G, 7ds, join to next picot of same ring, (3ds, p) four times, 7ds.
Rings F and G, Chain C, Rings A and B as before.
Chain A of 7ds, join to last picot of previous Chain A, 7ds, join to next picot of same chain, 7ds, join shuttle thread to Ring B, (7ds, p) twice, 7ds, rw.

Continue from Ring C as before.

Victorian Trefoil Edging

Using Coats *Chain* Mercer Crochet No. 40, the edging measures 4.5 cm (1¾ in in width.

Foundation row

Ring of (4ds, p) three times, 4ds, rw.
* Chain of 4ds, p, 4ds, rw.
Ring of 4ds, join to last picot of previous ring, (4ds, p) twice, 4ds, rw.

Repeat from * for the length required to the corner, ending with a ring. The total number of rings should be divisible by 5, plus an extra 3.

Corner chain of (4ds, p) three times, 4ds, rw.
Ring of 4ds, join to last picot of previous ring, 4ds, join to next picot of same ring, 4ds, p, 4ds, rw.

Repeat from * as before. The total number of rings after the corner chain should also be divisible by 5, plus an extra 3.

Second row

Ring A of 4ds, p, 4ds, join to first chain of foundation row, 4ds, p, 4ds, rw.
Chain A of 4ds, p, 4ds, rw.
Ring B of 4ds, join to previous ring, 4ds, join to next chain of foundation row, 4ds, p, 4ds, rw.
Work Chain A, Ring B once more.
* Chain B of (4ds, p) five times, 4ds, rw.
Ring A of 4ds, p, 4ds, miss the next chain of foundation row, and join to following chain, 4ds, p, 4ds, rw.
(Chain A, Ring B) three times.

Repeat from * all along the side, joining final Ring B to the first picot of corner chain.

Chain C of (4ds, p) seven times, 4ds, rw.
Ring A of 4ds, p, 4ds, join to last picot of corner chain, 4ds, p, 4ds, rw.
(Chain A, Ring B) three times.

Repeat from * as before.

Third row

Ring A of 4ds, p, 4ds, join to first Chain A of second row, 4ds, p, 4ds, rw.
* Chain A of 6ds, rw.
Ring B of 4ds, join to previous ring, 4ds, join to next Chain A of second row, 4ds, p, 4ds, rw.
Chain B of (4ds, p) three times, 4ds, rw.
Ring C of 4ds, join to previous ring, 4ds, miss first picot of Chain B of second row and join to the next, 4ds, p, 4ds, rw.
Chain C of 4ds, join to last picot of previous chain, (4ds, p) three times, 4ds, rw.
Ring D of 4ds, join to previous ring, 4ds, join to next picot of Chain B of second row, 4ds, p, 4ds, rw.
Work Chain C, Ring D once more.
Chain D of 4ds, join to last picot of previous chain, (4ds, p) twice, 4ds, rw.
Ring E of 4ds, join to previous ring, 4ds, join to next Chain A of second row, 4ds, p, 4ds, rw.
Chain E as Chain A.
Ring A of 4ds, join to previous ring, 4ds, join to next Chain A of second row, 4ds, p, 4ds, rw.
Repeat from * all along the side. At the corner work (Chain C, Ring D) four times, as shown.

Braids and strips

DAISY CHAIN

This intriguing chain cord, designed by Christine Appleton, is an example of Victorian Sets, also known as Twisted Tatting. It uses four shuttles, each wound with thread of a different colour. Each cluster of daisies completely surrounds the central cord. Using Coats *Chain* Mercer Crochet No. 20, the clusters measure 2 cm ($\frac{3}{4}$ in) in width.

Knot the four shuttle threads together.
* Select the shuttle with the colour required for the cord, and hold the remaining threads together firmly on the left hand:
Chain of 6 first-half stitches, 6 second-half stitches, *but retain the loop of the shuttle thread throughout*

Daisy Chain

and do not transfer it into a normal half stitch. Repeat four more times.

Select a shuttle for the first daisy:
Ring of 3ds, p, (2ds, p) five times, 3ds.
Take the remaining shuttles in turn and work a similar ring with each.

Repeat from * for the length required, holding the daisies out of the way when beginning a new chain. The length of each chain can be varied. The size and number of rings can also be varied: there is no need to use all the shuttles in every cluster.
Knot the four threads together to finish.

DIADEM

A prototype of this pattern was published by Eléonore Riego in *The Lace Tatting Book* (1866), and it has remained a favourite, with only slight variations in detail, ever since. Using Gütermann polyester top-stitching thread, the lace measures 2 cm ($\frac{3}{4}$ in) in width and will adapt to a curve.

Ring A of (4ds, p) twice, 4ds, rw.
* Chain A of 6ds.
Ring B of (2ds, p) ten times, 2ds, rw.
Chain B of 2ds, p, 2ds, join to last picot of Ring A, (2ds, p) twice, 2ds, rw.

Ring C of 4ds, miss last picot of Ring B and join to next picot, 4ds, rw.
Chain C of (2ds, p) four times, 2ds, rw.
Ring D of 4ds, miss next picot of Ring B and join to following picot, 4ds, rw.
Chain D of (2ds, p) four times, 2ds, miss next picot of Ring B and join shuttle thread to following picot, rw, 6ds, rw.
Ring A of 4ds, miss last picot of Chain D and join to following picot, 4ds, p, 4ds, rw.

Repeat from * for the length required.

Diadem

Using Coats *Chain* Mercer Crochet No. 20, the lace measures 4.5 cm (1¾ in), and requires two shuttles, wound on a continuous thread.

First row
Using main shuttle:
Ring A of 6ds, p, 2ds, p, 6ds, rw.
Chain A of 2ds, p, 6ds, join main shuttle thread to last picot of Ring A, turn work sideways.
* Chain B of 2ds, p, 6ds, join main shuttle thread to picot of Chain A, turn work sideways, 2ds.

Using second shuttle:
Ring B of (2ds, p) five times, 2ds.

Using main shuttle:
Chain C of 6ds, join main shuttle thread to picot of Chain B, rw.
Chain D of 6ds, p, 2ds, p, 6ds, join main shuttle

thread to base of same chain (in order to make a false ring), turn work sideways.
Chain A of 2ds, p, 6ds, join main shuttle thread to last picot of Chain D, turn work sideways.

Repeat from * for the length required, ending with Chain C.

Second row
Using shuttles as before:
Ring A of 6ds, join to free picot of Ring A of first row, 2ds, p, 6ds, rw.
* Chains A and B, Ring B, Chain C, as first row.
Chain D of 6ds, join to corresponding picot of Chain D of first row, 2ds, p, 6ds, join and turn as before.

Repeat from * all along, ending with Chain C.

Echo

Using Coats *Chain* Mercer Crochet No. 20, the braid measures 2 cm (¾ in) in width and will adapt to a curve.

* Ring A of 10ds, p, 5ds, p, 5ds, rw.
Chain A of 8ds, rw.
Ring B of 7ds, join to last picot of Ring A, 4ds, p, 4ds, rw.

Chain B of 6ds, rw.
Ring C of 4ds, join to Ring B, 4ds, rw.
Chain C of 10ds, p, 12ds, join shuttle thread to centre picot of Ring A, turn work sideways.
Chain D of 12ds, join shuttle thread to picot of Chain C.

Repeat from * for the length required.

Embryo

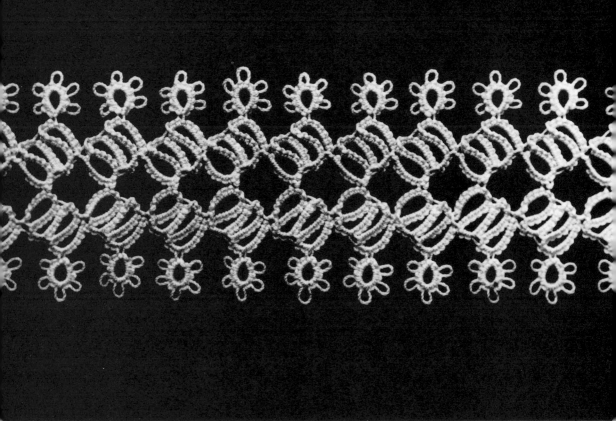

This is an example of Pearl Tatting, using two ball threads. Using Coats *Chain* Mercer Crochet No. 10, the braid measures 2.5 cm (1 in) in width and will adapt to a curve.

Knot together the two ball threads and the shuttle thread, and make a continuous chain:

Using ball A: 2ds, rw.
* Using ball B: space of 6 mm ($\frac{1}{4}$ in), 2ds, rw.
Using ball A: space of 6 mm, 2ds, rw.

Using ball B: space of 6 mm, 2ds, rw.
Using ball A: space of 6 mm, 3ds, p, 3ds, rw.
Using ball B: space of 3 mm, ($\frac{1}{8}$ in), 2ds, rw.
Using ball A: space of 6 mm, 2ds, rw.
Using ball B: space of 6 mm, 2ds, rw.
Using ball A: space of 6 mm, 2ds, rw.
Using ball B: space of 6 mm, 3ds, p, 3ds, rw.
Using ball A: space of 3 mm, 2ds, rw.

Repeat from * for the length required. Knot all threads together to finish.

Hopscotch

This pattern, with its interlocking clover shapes, was a well-used Edwardian classic. A short length, with tassels added at each end makes a pleasing bookmark. Using Coats Chain Mercer Crochet No. 20, the lace measures 3.5 cm (1$\frac{3}{8}$ in) in width.

First row
Ring A of (4ds, p) three times, 4ds.
* Ring B of 4ds, join to last picot of previous ring, (4ds, p) twice, 4ds.
Ring C of 4ds, join to last picot of previous ring, (4ds, p) twice, 4ds, rw.
Chain of 6ds, p, 4ds, p, 2ds, p, 4ds, p, 6ds, rw.
Ring A of 4ds, p, 4ds, join to centre picot of previous Ring C, 4ds, p, 4ds.

Repeat from * for the length required, ending with Ring C to complete the last clover.

Second row
Ring A of 4ds, p, 4ds, join to centre ring of last clover of first row, 4ds, p, 4ds.
* Ring B of 4ds, join to last picot of previous ring, 4ds, join to next junction between clovers, 4ds, p, 4ds.
Ring C of 4ds, join to previous ring, 4ds, join to centre ring of adjacent clover, 4ds, p, 4ds, rw.
Chain as in first row.
Ring A of 4ds, p, 4ds, join to junction of Ring C with centre ring, 4ds, p, 4ds.

Repeat from * all along, ending with Ring C as before.

Interlocking Clovers

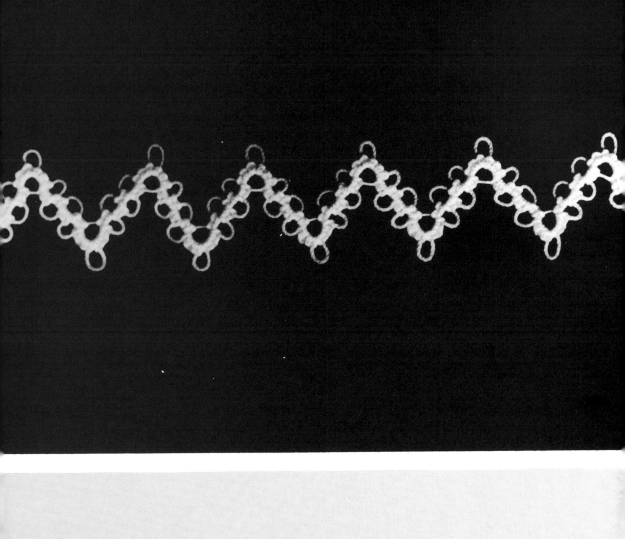

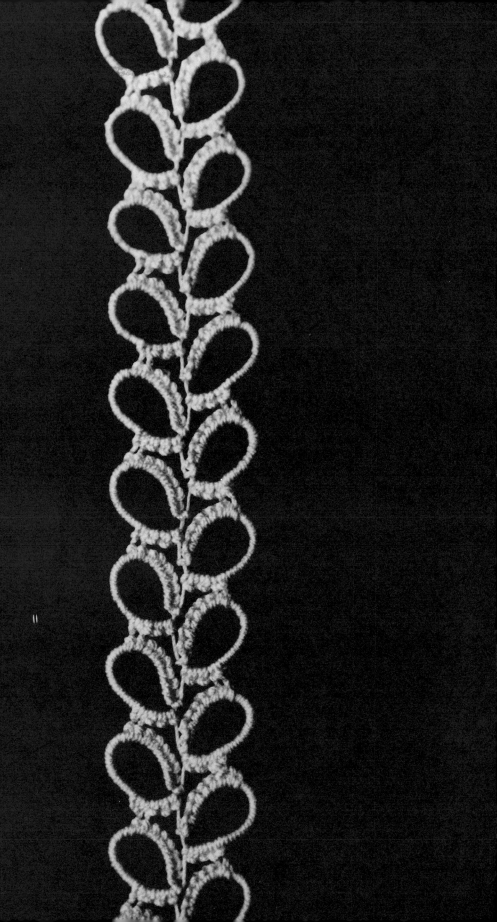

OLIVE BRANCH

Using Coats *Chain* Mercer Crochet No. 10, the braid measures 2 cm ($\frac{3}{4}$ in) in width, and is an example of Roll Tatting. Leave a very tiny space between each ring.

Ring A of 3ds, p, 1ds, 20rs, 1ds, p, 8ds, rw.
Ring B as Ring A.

* Ring A of 3ds, join to last picot of previous Ring A, 1ds, 20rs, 1ds, p, 8ds, rw.
Ring B of 3ds, join to last picot of previous Ring B, 1ds, 20rs, 1ds, p, 8ds, rw.

Repeat from * for the length required.

ROSEMARY

Using Coats *Chain* Mercer Crochet No. 20, the lace measures 2.5 cm (1 in) in width.

Ring A of 5ds, p, 2ds, p, 5ds.
Ring B of 5ds, join to last picot of previous ring, (2ds, p) five times, 5ds.
Ring C of 5ds, join to last picot of previous ring, 2ds, p, 5ds.
Ring D as Ring B.
Ring E of 5ds, join to last picot of previous ring, 2ds, p, 5ds, rw.

Repeat Rings A, B, C, D and E once more.
* Ring A of 5ds, join to last picot of adjacent Ring E, 2ds, p, 5ds.
Ring B of 5ds, join to last picot of previous ring, 2ds, join to corresponding picot of adjacent Ring D, (2ds, p) four times, 5ds.
Rings C, D and E as before.

Repeat from * for the length required.

SIMPLE SIMON†

This is the easiest pattern in the collection, and probably the most useful. Using Coats *Chain* Mercer Crochet No. 20, the braid measures 1.25 cm ($\frac{1}{2}$ in) in width and will adapt to a curve.

First ring of (2ds, p) five times, 3ds, p, (2ds, p) twice, 1ds.
* Holding the shuttle thread at back of work, leave a space equal to the height of the ring just made.

Ring of 2ds, join to fourth picot from end of the previous ring, (2ds, p) four times, 3ds, p, (2ds, p) twice, 1ds.

Repeat from * for the length required.

To curve the braid, shorten the spacing threads accordingly.

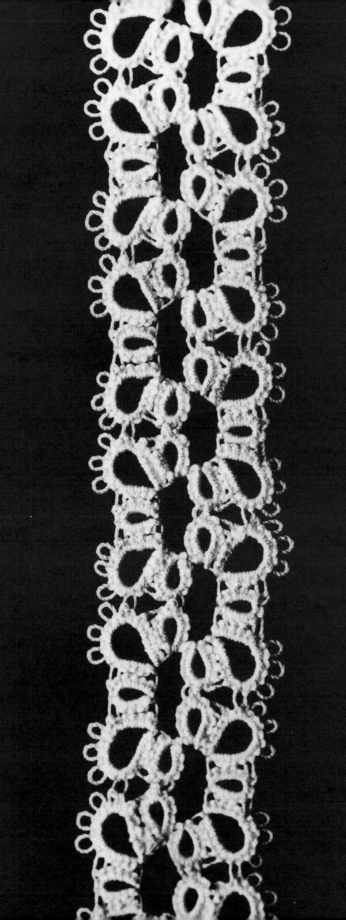

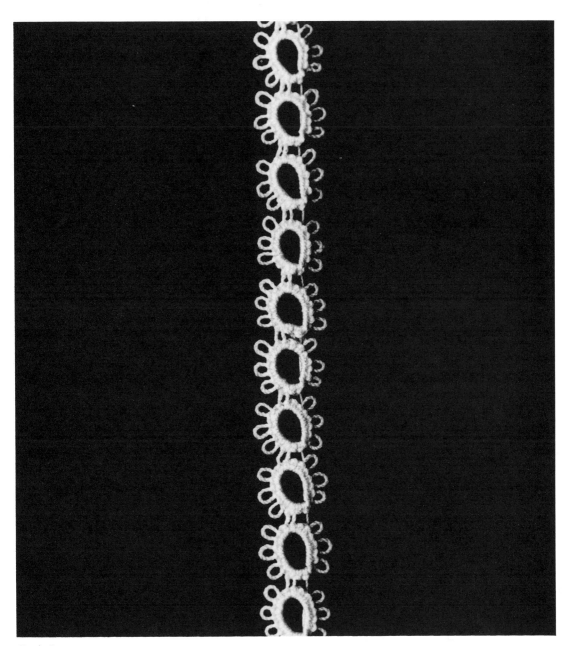

Simple Simon

Rosemary

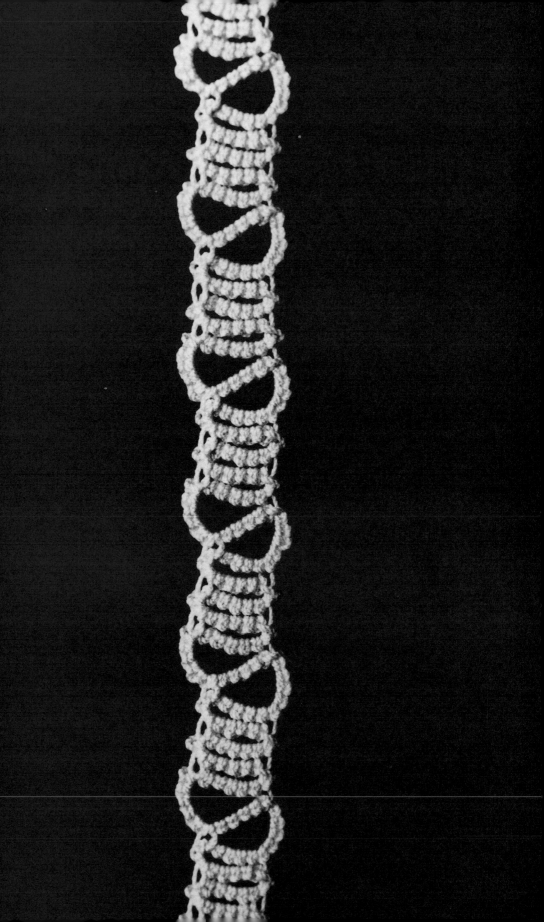

SNAKES AND LADDERS†

This pattern demonstrates how any thread which is too coarse or too brittle for use on the shuttle, can instead be used from the ball in conjunction with a more manageable shuttle thread. Metallic threads, and most knitting yarns, can be used in this way, using a finer crochet cotton on the shuttle. The threads chosen should match in colour. Using Twilley's *Crysette* from the ball, and Coats *Chain* Mercer Crochet No. 20 on the shuttle, the braid measures 2.5 cm (1 in) in width and will adapt to a curve.

Knot both threads together.
Chain A of 1ds, p, 5ds, rw.
* Chain B of 1ds, p, 5ds, join shuttle thread to picot of previous chain, turn work sideways.
Repeat Chain B three times more.
Chain C of 5ds, p, 5ds, join shuttle thread to picot of previous chain, turn work sideways.
Repeat Chain C once more.

Repeat from * for the length required, ending with Chain B.

SWEETHEARTS

This pattern, worked entirely in chains, is adapted from a specimen in *Beeton's Book of Needlework* (1870). Using Coats *Chain* Mercer Crochet No. 20, the tatting measures 3.5 cm ($1\frac{1}{4}$ in) in width.

Wind the shuttle directly from the ball and hang a saftey-pin on the thread as a convenient hold for starting the first chain.

First row
Chain A of 6ds, p, 6ds, p, 1ds, rw.
Chain B of 6ds, rw, join to last picot of Chain A, 6ds, p, 6ds, remove safety-pin and join shuttle thread to beginning of Chain A, rw.

* Chain C of 8ds, p, 8ds, p, 1ds, rw.
Chain A of 6ds, join to Chain B, 6ds, p, 1ds, rw.
Chain B of 6ds, rw, join to last picot of Chain A, 6ds, p, 6ds, join shuttle thread to last picot of Chain C, rw.

Repeat from * for the length required.

Second row
Chain A, Chain B as first row.
Chain C of 8ds, join to corresponding Chain C of first row, 8ds, p, 1ds, rw.
Complete as first row, joining every Chain C as shown.

SWEET PEA†

Using Coats *Chain* Mercer Crochet No. 20, the braid measures 2.5 cm (1 in) in width and will adapt to a curve.

Ring A of 7ds, p, 5ds, p, 3ds, p, 7ds.
* Ring B of 7ds, join to last picot of Ring A, 3ds, p, 10ds, rw.

Chain of 20ds, p, 5ds, join shuttle thread to picot of Ring B, 3ds.
Ring A of 7ds, join to picot of previous chain, 5ds, p, 3ds, p, 7ds.

Repeat from * for the length required.

WAVES†

Using Coats *Chain* Mercer Crochet No. 20, the braid measures 1.25 cm ($\frac{1}{2}$ in) in width and will adapt to a curve. This is a variation of Pearl Tatting, using two ball threads. Thread an equal number of small bugle beads on each ball.

Knot together the two ball threads and the shuttle thread.

Using ball A: Chain of (2ds, p) four times, 2ds, rw.
* Using ball B: Slip up a bead, chain of (2ds, p) four times, 2ds, rw.
Using ball A: Slip up a bead, chain of (2ds, p) four times, 2ds, rw.

Repeat from * for the length required. To finish, slip up the final bead and knot the ends together.

Waves

Sweet Pea

Sweethearts

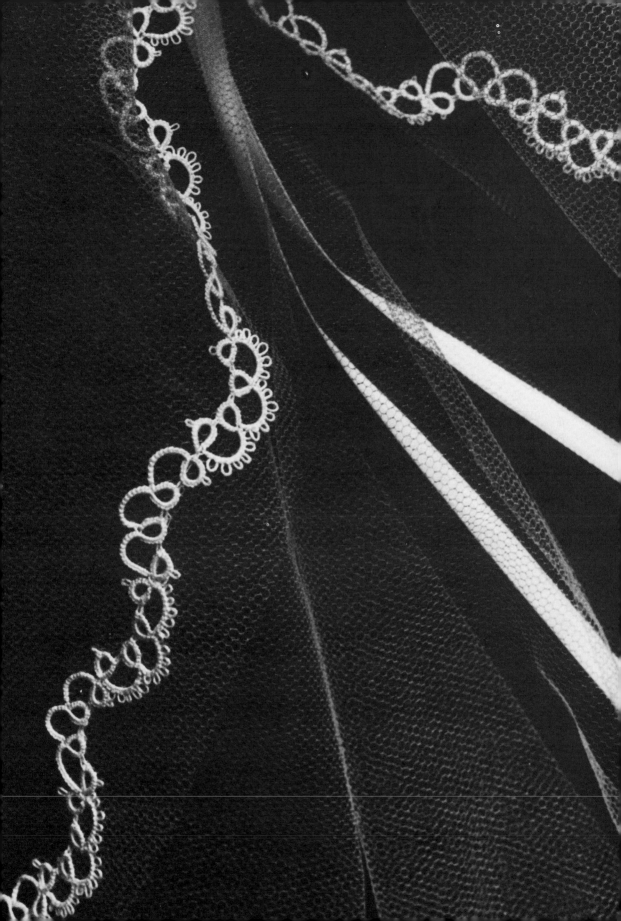

Composite designs

BRIDAL VEIL†

The tatting shown is attached to a circular veil but is equally suitable for a straight-edged rectangular veil. Using Coats *Chain* Mercer Crochet No. 60, the tatting measures 2 cm ($\frac{3}{4}$ in) in width. Using No. 40, it measures 2.5 cm (1 in). The diameter of the finished veil is 137 cm (54 in).

* Ring A of (6ds, p) twice, 6ds, rw.
Chain A of (2ds, p) 6 times, 2ds, rw.
Ring B of 6ds, join to last picot of previous ring, 6ds, p, 6ds, rw.
Work (Chain A, Ring B) twice more.
Ring A as before.
Chain B of 14ds, rw.
Ring B as before.
Work (Chain B, Ring B) twice more.

Repeat from * for approximately 432 cm (170 in), or the length required.

To prepare the net

Allow a 137 cm (54 in) square of bridal net. Fold it into quarters, giving a square of four layers. Pivot a tape-measure from the centre point as a guide to mark a curve, and cut a quarter circle.

To make up the veil

Press the tatting under a damp cloth. Attach it to the net, leaving a margin of 1.25 cm ($\frac{1}{2}$ in) from the cut edge of the net, using fine sewing cotton. Sew the tatting invisibly into place from the *back* of the work, stitching through each junction of the rings and leaving the chains free. Press the finished veil lightly.

Using Coats *Chain* Mercer Crochet No. 20, the collar measures 7.5 cm (3 in) in width. The length and curvature are adjustable.

First motif

Ring A of 6ds, p, 4ds, p, (2ds, p) twice, 4ds, p, 6ds, rw.
Chain A of (4ds, p) three times, 4ds, rw.
Ring B of 6ds, join to last picot of previous ring, 4ds, join to next picot of same ring, (2ds, p) twice, 4ds, p, 6ds, rw.
Chain B of 4ds, p, 4ds, rw.
Ring B as before.
Chain C of (6ds, p) twice, 4ds, rw.
Ring B as before, but do not reverse work.
Chain D of 6ds, rw.
Ring C of 4ds, join to last picot of Chain C, (4ds, p) twice, 4ds.
Chain E of 4ds, join to last picot of previous ring, 4ds, p, 4ds.
Ring D of 4ds, join to previous chain, 8ds, p, 6ds, p, 6ds, rw.
Chain F of 6ds, rw.
Ring E of (6ds, p) twice, 8ds, p, 4ds.
Chain G as Chain E.
Ring F of 4ds, join to previous chain, (4ds, p) twice, 4ds, rw.
Chain H of 6ds.
Ring B of 6ds, join to last picot of previous Ring B, 4ds, join to next picot of same ring, (2ds, p) twice, 4ds, p, 6ds, rw.
Chain I of 4ds, join to last picot of Ring F, 6ds, p, 6ds, rw.
Ring B as before.
Chain J as Chain B.
Ring B and Chain A as before.
Ring B of 6ds, join to last picot of previous Ring B, 4ds, join to next picot of same ring, 2ds, p, 2ds, join to corresponding picot of Ring A at beginning, 4ds, join to next picot of same ring, 6ds, rw.
Chain A as before.
Tie to base of Ring A to finish.

Second motif

Work Ring A, Chain A, Ring B as first motif.
Chain B of 4ds, join to Chain J of first motif, 4ds, rw.
Ring B as before.
Chain C of 6ds, join to corresponding picot of Chain I of first motif, 6ds, p, 4ds, rw.
Ring B and Chain D as before.
Ring C of 4ds, join to Chain C, 4ds, join to Ring F of first motif, 4ds, p, 4ds.
Chain E as before.
Ring D of 4ds, join to Chain E, 8ds, join to corresponding picot of Ring E of first motif, 6ds, p, 6ds.
Complete the remainder as first motif.

Join a series of sixteen motifs, or the number required.

Inner edging

Ring of 8ds, join to first picot at neck edge of collar, 4ds, p, 8ds, p, 4ds. Leave a space of 6 mm ($\frac{1}{4}$ in).
* Ring A of 4ds, join to second picot from end of previous ring, (4ds, p) twice, 8ds, p, 4ds. Space as before.
Ring B of 4ds, join to second picot from end of previous ring, 4ds, join to next picot at neck edge, 4ds, p, 8ds, p, 4ds. Space as before.
Work Ring B once more. Space as before.

Repeat from * till the final ring is reached.
Final ring of 4ds, join to second picot from end of previous ring, 4ds, join to last picot at neck edge, 12ds, p, 4ds.

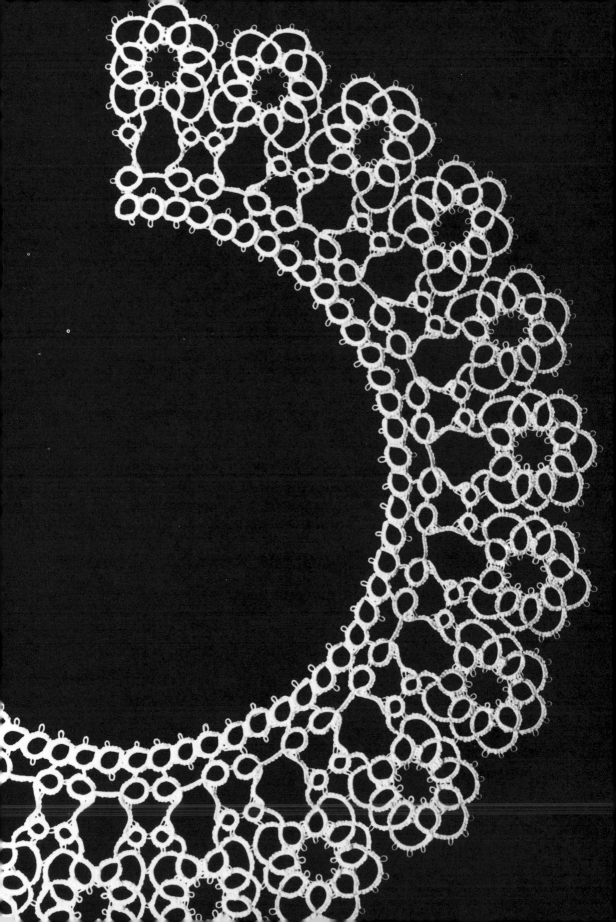

Using Coats *Chain* Mercer Crochet No. 20, the edging measures 6.5 cm ($2\frac{1}{2}$ in) in width, and the completed mat is 36 cm ($14\frac{1}{4}$ in) in diameter.

Join a circle of 24 motifs as given for the circular collar. Omit the inner edging.

To make up
Shrink and press both the tatting and the fabric.

Using a plate or similar article of 23 cm (9 in) diameter as a template, draw a circle on the fabric using a pencil. Run a tacking thread as a stay just inside the pencil line. Cut the fabric to within 2 cm ($\frac{3}{4}$ in) of the pencil line.

Turn back a single fold along the stay thread and tack into place.
Using a crochet hook, size 1 mm, work double crochet over the fold, inserting the hook through the two layers of fabric. Cut away excess fabric at the back afterwards.

Using matching sewing cotton, overcast the edge of the double crochet, picking up picots from the tatting as necessary.

FLOWER PATCH

Most machine-made, floral laces will take an encrustation of tatting as shown here. The tatted florets can be attached in clusters, or singly, according to the requirements of the fabric. Equally, the method can be used for floral satins and many other dress fabrics. Using Coats *Chain* Mercer Crochet No. 20, the large florets measure 2.25 cm ($\frac{7}{8}$ in) in diameter. Using No. 40, the small florets measure 1.25 cm ($\frac{1}{2}$ in) in diameter.

Make several florets of each size before planning the appliqué, and leave ends of approximately 15 cm (6 in) for sewing.

Large floret
Ring of 9ds, p, 11ds, p, 9ds.

* Ring of 9ds, join to last picot of previous ring, 11ds, p, 9ds.
Repeat from * three times more.
Ring of 9ds, join to previous ring, 11ds, join to corresponding picot of first ring, 9ds.
Tie the two ends together to finish.

Small floret
Ring of 7ds, p, 9ds, p, 7ds.
* Ring of 7ds, join to last picot of previous ring, 9ds, p, 7ds.
Repeat from * once more.
Ring of 7ds, join to previous ring, 9ds, join to corresponding picot of first ring, 7ds.
Tie the two ends together to finish.

Three matching mats of differing sizes are the basis of this beautiful set, also shown on page 6. The design is from *Penelope Book 3*, published in the 1950s. One mat of each size can be made from two 20 g balls of the cotton specified. Using Coats *Chain Mercer Crochet No. 20*, the mat measures 35 cm (14 in) in diameter.

First round

Ring A of (3ds, p) five times, 3ds.
Ring B of 3ds, join to last picot of previous ring, (3ds, p) six times, 3ds.
Ring C of 3ds, join to last picot of previous ring, (3ds, p) four times, 3ds, rw.
Chain of 8ds, p, 3ds, p, (1ds, p) twice, 3ds, p, 8ds, rw.
* Ring A of (3ds, p) twice, 3ds, join to third picot from the end of previous ring, (3ds, p) twice, 3ds.
Rings B and C as before.
Chain of 8ds, join to last picot of previous chain, 3ds, p, (1ds, p) twice, 3ds, p, 8ds, rw.

Repeat from * six times more, joining final Ring C to first Ring A, and final chain to first to complete the round. Tie to base of first ring to finish.

Second round

* Ring of (3ds, p) twice, 3ds, join to fourth free picot (counting in the order worked) of first Ring B of previous round, (3ds, p) twice, 3ds, rw.
Chain A of (3ds, p) three times, 3ds, rw.
Ring of (3ds, p) twice, 3ds, join to second free picot of same Ring B, (3ds, p) twice, 3ds, rw.
Chain B of (3ds, p) three times, (1ds, p) twice, (3ds, p) twice, 3ds, rw.

Repeat from * all around, joining to each Ring B in turn. Tie final Chain B to base of first ring to finish.

Third round

Join to centre picot of first Chain A of previous round.
* Chain of 3ds, p) three times, 3ds, join shuttle thread to second picot of next Chain B.
Chain of (3ds p) three times, 3ds, join shuttle thread to sixth picot of same chain.
Chain of (3ds, p) three times, join shuttle thread to centre picot of next Chain A.

Repeat from * all round. Tie to base of first chain to finish.

Fourth round

Join to centre picot of first chain of previous round.
* Chain of (4ds, p) three times, 4ds, join shuttle thread to centre picot of next chain.

Repeat from * all round. Tie to base of first chain to finish.

Fifth round

Rings A, B and C as beginning of first round.
Chain A of 8ds, p, (3ds, p) twice, 3ds, join to centre picot of first chain of previous round, (3ds, p) twice, 3ds, rw.
* Ring D of (3ds, p) twice, 3ds, join to third picot from the end of previous Ring C, (3ds, p) twice, 3ds.
Ring E of (3ds, p) five times, 3ds, rw.
Chain B of (3ds, p) twice, 3ds, join to centre picot of next chain of previous round, (3ds, p) three times, 8ds, rw.
Ring A of (3ds, p) twice, 3ds, join to centre picot of previous Ring E, (3ds, p) twice, 3ds.
Rings B and C as before.
Chain A of 8ds, join to last picot of Chain B, (3ds, p) twice, 3ds, join to centre picot of next chain of previous round, (3ds, p) twice, 3ds, rw.

Repeat from * all round, joining final Ring E to first Ring A, and final Chain B to first Chain A. Tie to base of first ring to finish.

Sixth round

* Ring of (3ds, p) twice, 3ds, join to last free picot (counting in the order worked) of first Ring B of previous round, (3ds, p) twice, 3ds, rw.
Chain A of (3ds, p) three times, 3ds, rw.
Ring of (3ds, p) twice, 3ds, join to centre free picot of same Ring B, (3ds, p) twice, 3ds, rw.

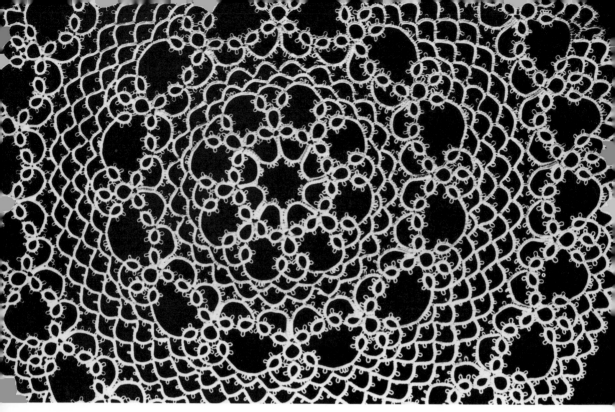

Chain A as before.

Ring of (3ds, p) twice, 3ds, join to first free picot of same Ring B, (3ds, p) twice, 3ds, rw.

Chain B of (3ds, p) 3 times, (1ds, p) twice (3ds, p) twice, 3ds, rw.

Repeat from * all round, joining to each Ring B in turn. Tie final Chain B to base of first ring to finish.

Seventh round

Join to centre picot of first Chain A of previous round.

* Chain of (3ds, p) three times, 3ds, join shuttle thread to centre picot of next Chain A.

Chain as before, join shuttle thread to second picot of next Chain B.

Chain as before, join shuttle thread to sixth picot of same Chain B.

Chain as before, join shuttle thread to centre picot of next Chain A.

Repeat from * all round. Tie to base of first chain to finish.

finish.

Eighth to tenth rounds

As fourth round.

Eleventh round

As fifth round.

Twelfth round

As sixth round.

Thirteenth round

As seventh round.

Fourteenth round

Join to centre picot of any chain of previous round.

* Chain of (3ds, p) twice, (1ds, p) twice, 3ds, p, 3ds, join shuttle thread to centre picot of next chain.

Repeat from * all round. Tie to base of first chain to finish.

Press accurately under a damp cloth.

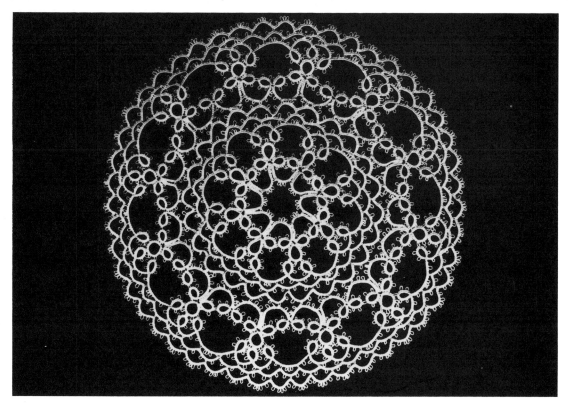

Hostess Set: Place mat

HOSTESS SET: PLACE MAT ———————————

Using Coats *Chain* Mercer Crochet No. 20, the mat measures 23 cm (9 in) in diameter.

Work first to seventh rounds as given for the centrepiece, then work the fourteenth round to finish.

HOSTESS SET: GLASS MAT ———————————

Using Coats *Chain* Mercer Crochet No. 20, the mat measures 12.5 cm (5 in) in diameter.

Work first to third rounds as given for the centrepiece, then work the fourteenth round to finish.

Hostess Set: Glass mat

Using Coats *Chain* Mercer Crochet No. 20, the mat measures 26 cm (10¼ in) in diameter.

Centre motif

With shuttle wound directly from the ball:
Ring of (9ds, p) twice, 9ds.
*Ring of 9ds, join to last picot of previous ring, 9ds, p, 9ds.

Repeat from * 5 times more.
Ring of 9ds, join to last picot of previous ring, 9ds, join to first picot of first ring, 9ds.
Tie both threads together at back of work, then join the shuttle thread to junction of first and last rings. Take the ball thread to same junction.

Chain A of (11ds, join shuttle thread to next junction of rings, small p) eight times.
Chain B of (13ds, join shuttle thread to next small picot of previous chain, small p) eight times.
Chain C of (15ds, join shuttle thread to next small picot of previous chain, small p) eight times.
Chain D of (3ds, p, 4ds, p, 3ds, p, 4ds, p, 3ds, join shuttle thread to next small picot of previous chain) eight times.
Tie ends to finish.

Centre round

Ring A of 9ds, p, (4ds, p) twice, 9ds.
* Ring B of 9ds, join to last picot of previous ring, 2ds, p, 4ds, p, 2ds, p, 9ds.
Ring C as Ring B.
Ring D as Ring B.
Ring E of 9ds, join to last picot of previous ring, (4ds, p) twice, 9ds, rw.
Chain of 7ds, join to second picot (counting in the order worked) of Chain D of centre motif, 4ds, join to first picot of same chain, 7ds, join shuttle thread to last picot of Ring E, 7ds, join to next picot of centre motif, 4ds, join to following picot of centre motif, 7ds, rw.
Ring A of 9ds, join to junction of last Ring E with chain, 4ds, join to next picot of Ring E, 4ds, p, 9ds.
Repeat from * all around, joining final Ring E to first Ring A.

Tie final chain to base of first Ring A to finish.

'Mist' border: first round

Ring of 4ds, join to any free picot of centre round, 4ds. Space of 1 cm (⅜ in).
* Ring of 4ds, join to next free picot of centre round, 4ds. Space as before.
Repeat from * all around.

Second round

* Ring of 4ds, join to next space of previous round, 4ds. Space as before.
Repeat from * all around.

Third to fifth rounds

As second round.

Sixth round

* Ring of 4ds, join to next space of previous round, 4ds. Space as before.
Ring of 4ds, join to same space of previous round, 4ds. Space as before.
Ring of 4ds, join to next space of previous round, 4ds. Space as before.
Repeat from * all around.

Seventh to tenth rounds

As second round.

Eleventh round

* Ring of 4ds, join to next space of previous round, 4ds, rw. Space of 6 mm (¼ in).
Ring of 8ds, rw. Space as before.
Repeat from * all around. Tie to first space to finish.

LOVE-IN-A-MIST: GLASS MAT

Using Coats *Chain* Mercer Crochet No. 20, the mat measures 15 cm (6 in) in diameter.

Work centre motif and centre round as place mat. Then work first to third rounds only of the 'Mist' border, working the eleventh round to finish.

Love-in-a-mist: Glass mat

These hexagonal motifs can be assembled in inter-locking rows to form a rectangular cloth, or in concentric rounds to form a six-sided cloth. Using Coats *Chain* Mercer Crochet No. 20, the motif measures 5 cm (2 in) across.

First motif

Ring A of 6ds, p, 3ds, p, 3ds.
Chain A of 5ds, rw.
Ring B of (3ds, p) five times, 3ds, rw.
* Chain B of 5ds.
Ring C of 3ds, join to last picot of previous Ring A, 3ds, p, 6ds, rw.
Chain C of 5ds, join to last picot of previous Ring B, 4ds, p, 5ds, rw.
Ring A, Chain A as before.
Ring B of 3ds, join to last picot of previous Chain C, 3ds, join to corresponding picot of Ring B, (3ds, p) three times, 3ds rw.

Repeat from * four times more, joining final Ring B to the first.
Chain B, Ring C as before.
Chain C of 5ds, join to last Ring B, 4ds, join to first Ring B, 5ds.
Tie to base of first Ring A to finish.

Second motif

Ring A, Chain A, Ring B, Chain B as before.
Ring C of 3ds, join to last picot of previous Ring A, 3ds, join to corresponding ring of first motif, 6ds, rw.
Chain C as before.
Ring A of 6ds, join to corresponding ring of first motif, 3ds, p, 3ds.
Continue from Chain A, and complete as first motif.

Join further motifs as shown.

Mosaic

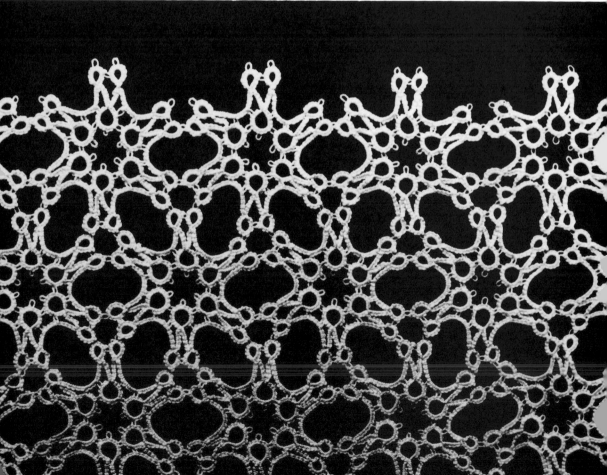

Only the tiny centre rings are true rings: the rest of the tatting is worked in chains. Using Coats *Chain* Mercer Crochet No. 20, the motif measures 7 cm ($2\frac{3}{4}$ in) across.

First motif
First round:
Centre ring of 3ds, p, 6ds, p, 3ds, rw.
Chain A of 5ds, p, (9ds, p) three times, 5ds, rw.
* Centre ring of 3ds, join to last picot of previous centre ring, 6ds, p, 3ds, rw.
Chain A of 5ds, join to last picot of previous Chain A, (9ds, p) three times, 5ds, rw.

Repeat from * three times more.
Centre ring of 3ds, join to previous centre ring, 6ds, join to first centre ring, 3ds, rw.
Chain A of 5ds, join to previous Chain A, (9ds, p) twice, 9ds, join to first Chain A, 5ds.
Making sure that both threads remain at the back of work, join shuttle thread to base of first centre ring, then join shuttle thread to junction of first and last Chains A.

Second round:
Chain B of 9ds, join shuttle thread to next picot of Chain A.
Chain C of 9ds, p, 3ds, p, 9ds, join shuttle thread to same picot—this makes a false ring.
* Chain D of 9ds, join shuttle thread to next picot of Chain A.
Chain E of 9ds, p, 3ds, p, 9ds, join shuttle thread to same picot.
Chain F of 9ds, join shuttle thread to next junction between Chains A.
Chain B as before.
Chain C of 9ds, join to last picot of previous Chain E, 3ds, p, 9ds, join shuttle thread as before.

Repeat from * all around, joining final false ring to the first, and ending with Chain F. Tie to junction of Chains A to finish.

Second motif
Work first round, and first Chain B of second round, as before.
Chain C of 9ds, p, 3ds, join to corresponding false ring of first motif, 9ds, join shuttle thread as before.
Chain D as before.
Chain E of 9ds, join to corresponding false ring of first motif, 3ds, p, 9ds, join shuttle thread as before.
Continue from Chain F, and complete as first motif.

Join further motifs as shown, and see also the introductory text to *Mosaic*. Press well on completion.

ROSE COLLAR

Most tatted collars are circular, but this one has been specially designed for a V-shaped neckline. The length and curvature are adjustable. Using Coats *Chain* Mercer Crochet No. 20, the collar measures 7 cm ($2\frac{3}{4}$ in) in width.

First motif
With shuttle wound directly from the ball:
Centre ring of (3ds, p) seven times, 3ds. Work lock stitch to form an eighth false picot.
Chain A of (5ds, join shuttle thread to next picot of centre ring, small p) eight times.
Chain B of (7ds, join shuttle thread to next small picot of Chain A, small p) eight times.
Chain C of (9ds, join shuttle thread to next small picot of Chain B, small p) eight times.
Chain D of (5ds, p, 5ds, join shuttle thread to next small picot of Chain C) eight times, 5ds, join shuttle thread to first picot of round.
* Chain E of 9ds, p, 9ds, join shuttle thread to same picot—thus making a 'leaf'.
Chain F of 15ds, join shuttle thread to next picot of Chain D.

Repeat from * four times more, then work Chain E once more.

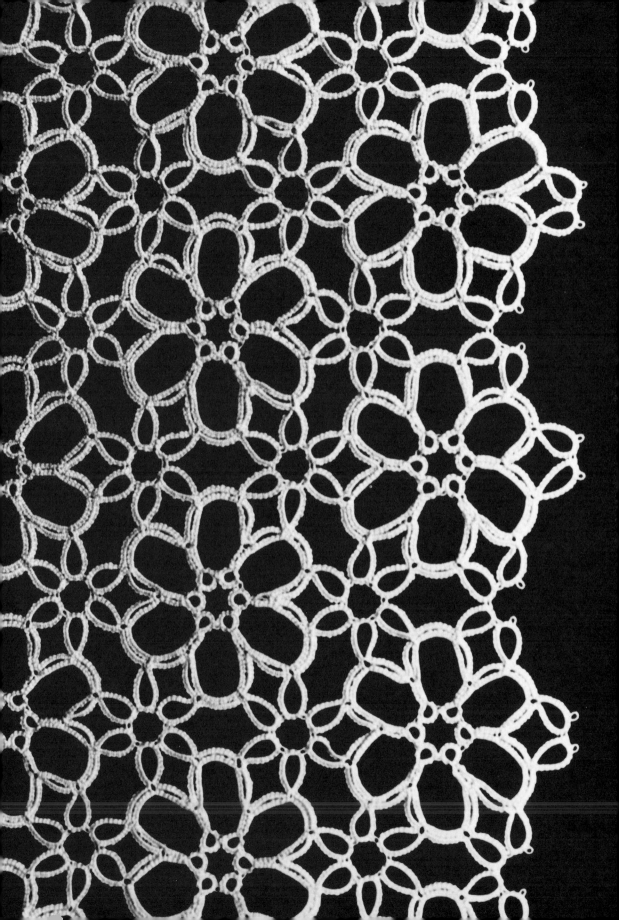

Chain G of 5ds, join shuttle thread to next junction on Chain D, rw.

Chain H of 9ds, p, 7ds, rw.

Ring A of 9ds, join to last 'leaf', 9ds.

Chain I of 7ds, p, 7ds, p, 5ds.

Ring B of 4ds, p, 5ds, p, 9ds, rw.

Chain J of 9ds, join to Chain H, 9ds, join to next junction on Chain D, 9ds, p, 9ds, rw.

Ring C of 9ds, join to corresponding picot of Ring B, 5ds, p, 4ds.

Chain K of 5ds, p, 7ds, p, 7ds, rw.

Ring D of 9ds, join to first 'leaf' after twisting the 'leaf' forward and downwards, 9ds.

Chain L of 7ds, join to Chain J, 9ds—this join should have negated the 'leaf' twist.

Tie to next junction on Chain D to finish.

Second motif

Work as first motif until the fifth 'leaf' is reached.

Chain E of 9ds, join to second 'leaf' of first motif (counting in the order worked), 9ds, join shuttle thread as before.

Chain F as before.

Chain E of 9ds, join to junction of 'leaf' and ring of first motif, 9ds, join shuttle thread as before.

Chains G and H as before.

Ring A of 9ds, join to junction of 'leaves' and ring, 9ds.

Chain I of 7ds, join to Chain K of first motif, 7ds, p, 5ds.

Complete the remainder as first motif.

Join a series of seven motifs (or the number required) for each half-collar.

Inner edging

Ring of 5ds, join to first picot on inner edge, 5ds, p, 9ds, rw.

Chain of 11ds, join shuttle thread to picot of ring just made, rw.

* Ring of 5ds, join to next picot on inner edge, 5ds, p, 9ds, rw.

Chain as before.

Repeat from * along four motifs, or for the length required for a straight edge.

To curve the collar, continue with:

* Ring of 4ds, join to next picot on inner edge, 4ds, p, 7ds, rw.

Chain of 9ds, join shuttle thread to picot of ring just made, rw.

Repeat from * to end of row.

Work the second half-collar to match.

Rose Collar: detail   Rose Collar

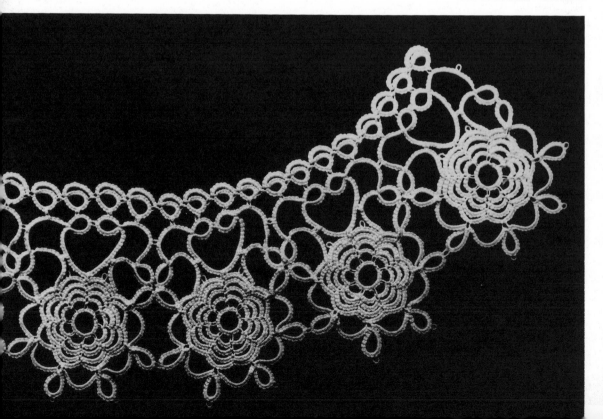

Using Coats *Chain* Mercer Crochet No. 20, the motif measures 8.5 cm (3¼ in) across.

First Motif

Ring A of 8ds, p, 8ds, rw.

Chain A of 4ds, p, 8ds, p, (4ds, p) twice, 8ds, p, 4ds, rw.

* Ring B of 8ds, join to previous Ring A, 8ds, rw.

Chain B of 4ds, rw.

Ring C as Ring A.

Chain C of 10ds, join shuttle thread to picot of Ring C, small p, 10ds, join shuttle thread to base of Ring C, rw.

Chain D of (4ds, p) three times, 2ds, join shuttle thread to small picot of Chain C, 2ds, (p, 4ds) three times, join shuttle thread to base of Ring C, rw.

Chain E of 4ds, rw.

Ring A as before.

Chain A of 4ds, join to last picot of previous Chain A, 8ds, join to next picot of same chain, (4ds, p) twice, 8ds, p, 4ds, rw.

Repeat from * three times more, then work from Ring B to Ring A once more.

Chain A of 4ds, join to last picot of previous Chain A, 8ds, join to next picot of same chain, 4ds, p, 4ds, join to corresponding picot of first Chain A, 8ds, join to corresponding picot of same chain, 4ds, rw.

Work from Ring B to Chain E as before.

Tie to base of first Ring A to finish.

Second motif

Work as first motif till first Chain C has been worked.

Chain D of (4ds, p) three times, 2ds, join shuttle thread to small picot of Chain C, 2ds, join to corresponding picot of any Chain D of first motif, (4ds, p) twice, 4ds, join shuttle thread to base of Ring C, rw.

Work from Chain E to Chain C as before.

Chain D of (4ds, p) twice, 4ds, join to corresponding picot of next Chain D of first motif, 2ds, join shuttle thread to small picot of Chain C, 2ds, (p, 4ds) three times, join shuttle thread to base of Ring C, rw.

Continue from Chain E and complete as first motif.

Join further motifs as shown; see also the introductory text to *Mosaic*.

Designed for a hymnal or prayer book, this cover features the classic four-four pattern, arranged in strips. It is adaptable for a book of any size. Using Coats *Chain* Mercer Crochet No. 20, each strip measures 2.5 cm (1 in) in width.

First strip
First row:
Ring of (4ds, p) three times, 4ds, rw.
* Chain of 4ds, p, 4ds, rw.
Ring of 4ds, join to last picot of previous ring, (4ds, p) twice, 4ds, rw.

Repeat from * for the length required for the height of the book, ending with a ring. Do not reverse work after the last ring.
Turning chain of 4ds, p, 4ds.
Second row:
Ring of (4ds, p) three times, 4ds, rw.
* Chain of 4ds, join to corresponding chain of first row, 4ds, rw.
Ring of 4ds, join to last picot of previous ring, (4ds, p) twice, 4ds, rw.
Repeat from * all along the row, ending with a ring. Do not reverse work after the last ring, but work a turning chain as before. Tie to beginning of first row to finish.

Second strip
First row:
Ring of 4ds, p, 4ds, join to corresponding picot of last ring of first strip, 4ds, p, 4ds, rw.
* Chain of 4ds, p, 4ds, rw.

Ring of 4ds, join to last picot of previous ring, 4ds, join to next ring of first strip, 4ds, p, 4ds, rw.

Repeat from * all along the row. Turn, and complete as first strip.

Join sufficient strips to cover the book, allowing three extra strips for each inside flap.

Edgings
Fold each inside flap so that its picots coincide with those of the outer cover. The top and bottom edgings are alike and are worked from fold to fold, joining the double layers of tatting together. The double-layered picots are used together, as single picots.

With shuttle wound directly from the ball, tie to first picot:
* Chain of 4ds, p, 4ds, join shuttle thread to next picot.
Repeat from * all along the edge. Tie final chain to last picot.

On completion, damp the tatting thoroughly to shrink it for a perfect fit.

Ribbon trimmings (make two)
Work a very short strip (as given for first strip), with two rings only in each row.

Thread the trimmings on a ribbon as shown.

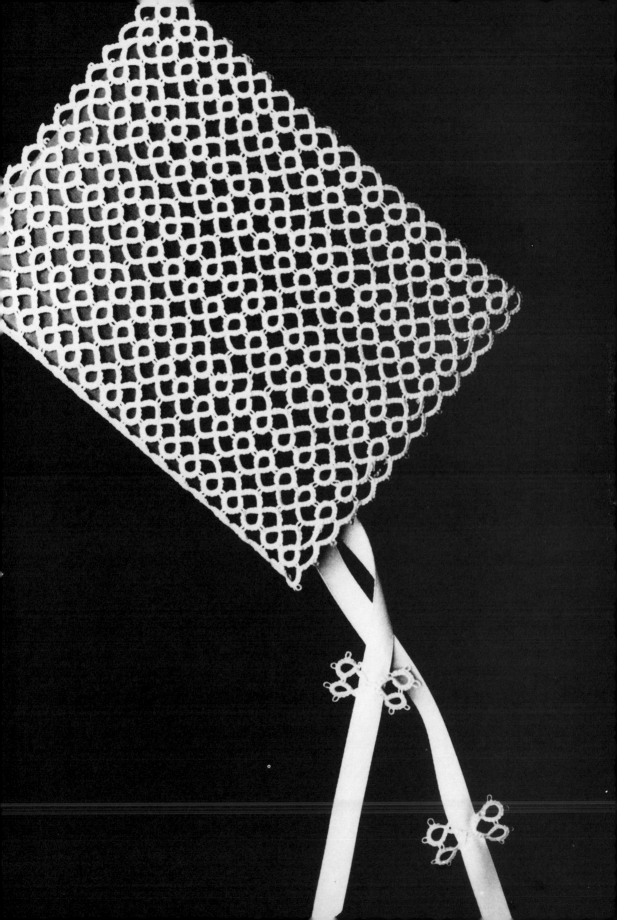

This design was given originally as a luncheon set in Coats' *Learn Tatting*, published in the 1960s. Using Coats *Chain* Mercer Crochet No. 20, the motif measures 5 cm (2 in) square. A mat size 30 cm × 46 cm (12 in × 18 in), assembled from 54 motifs, requires two 20 g balls.

First motif

Ring A of 7ds, p, 7ds.
Ring B of 7ds, large p, 7ds.
* Ring C of 7ds, p, 7ds, rw.
Chain A of 5ds, p, 5ds.
Ring D of 6ds, p, (5ds, p) twice, 6ds.
Chain B of 5ds, join shuttle thread to previous Ring C, 5ds.
Ring E of 6ds, join to last picot of Ring D, (5ds, p) twice, 6ds.
Chain C of 5ds, p, 5ds, rw.
Ring A of 7ds, join to junction of Ring C with Chain B, 7ds.

Ring B of 7ds, join to large picot at centre, 7ds.
Repeat from * twice more.
Ring C of 7ds, join to first Ring A, 7ds, rw.
Chain A, Ring D, Chain B, Ring E and Chain C as before.
Tie to base of first Chain A to finish.

Second motif

Rings A, B, C, Chain A, Ring D and Chain B as before.
Ring E of 6ds, join to last picot of Ring D, 5ds, join to corresponding picot of any Ring D of first motif, 5ds, join to next picot of same ring, 6ds.
Chain C, Rings A, B, C and Chain A as before.
Ring D of 6ds, join to corresponding picot of adjacent Ring E of first motif, 5ds, join to next picot of same ring, 5ds, p, 6ds.
Continue from Chain B and complete as first motif.

Join further motifs in rows as shown.

Individual designs and fragments

ALMONDS

This is an example of Roll Tatting. Using Coats *Chain* Mercer Crochet No. 20, the tatting measures 4.5 cm ($1\frac{3}{4}$ in) in height, using No. 60 it measures 3.5 cm ($1\frac{1}{4}$ in).

First motif

Ring A of 1ds, 20rs, 1ds, p, 4ds, p, 6ds, rw.
Ring B of 6ds, p, 6ds, rw.
Ring C of 6ds, join to last picot of Ring A, 6ds, rw.
Ring D of 6ds, join to Ring B, 1ds, 24rs, 1ds, p, 6ds, rw.
Ring E as Ring B.

Ring F of 6ds, join to Ring D, 6ds, rw.
Ring G of 6ds, join to Ring E, 4ds, p, 1ds, 20rs, 1ds.
Cut thread and finish.

Second motif

Ring A of 1ds, 20rs, 1ds, join to Ring G of first motif, 4ds, p, 6ds, rw.
Rings B to F as before.
Ring G of 6ds, join to Ring E, 4ds, join to Ring A of first motif, 1ds, 20rs, 1ds.
Cut thread and finish.

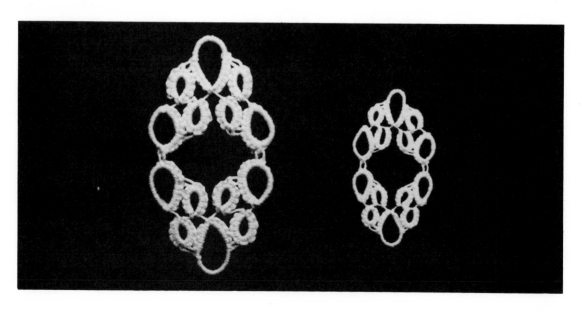

BACKCHAT

Using Coats *Chain* Mercer Crochet No. 20, the tatting measures 7.5 cm (3 in) in width. Two shuttles are needed, wound on a continuous thread.

First spray

Using main shuttle:
Ring A of (4ds, p) five times, 4ds, rw.
Chain A of 10ds, p, 2ds, join main shuttle thread to last picot of Ring A.
Chain B of 2ds, join to previous chain, 8ds, p, 2ds, join main shuttle thread to next picot of Ring A.
Chain C of 2ds, join to previous chain, (6ds, p) twice, 2ds, join main shuttle thread to next picot of Ring A.
Repeat Chain C twice more.
Chain D of 2ds, join to last picot of previous chain, 4ds, p, 2ds, p, 10ds, rw.
Ring B of 10ds, join to junction of Chains A and B, 5ds, p, 5ds, rw.

Using second shuttle:
Ring C of 7ds, p, 7ds.

Using main shuttle:
Chain E of 6ds, p, 4ds, p, 5ds, p, 5ds, rw.
Ring D of 10ds, join to junction of Chains B and C, 5ds, p, 5ds, rw.

Using second shuttle:
Ring E of 5ds, join to last picot of Chain E, 5ds, p, 10ds, rw.

Using main shuttle:
Chain F of 6ds, p, 6ds, rw.
Ring F of 7ds, join to Ring E, 4ds, p, 6ds.
Tie ends to finish.

Second spray

Using main shuttle:
Ring A, Chains A, B and C as before.
Repeat Chain C once more.
Final Chain C of 2ds, join to previous chain, 6ds, join to corresponding Chain C of first spray, 6ds, p, 2ds, join shuttle thread to next picot of Ring A.
Chain D of 2ds, join to previous chain, 4ds, join to corresponding picot of Chain D of first spray, 2ds, join to next picot of same chain, 10ds, rw.
Ring B as before.

Using second shuttle:
Ring C of 7ds, join to Ring C of first spray, 7ds.

Complete the remainder as first spray.

Using Coats *Chain* Mercer Crochet No. 20, the lace measures 5.5 cm (2$\frac{1}{4}$ in) in width. Leave a space of 3 mm ($\frac{1}{8}$ in) between all rings, and gradate the lengths of picots on Rings B and H as shown.

Ring A of 6ds, p, 6ds, rw.
Ring B of 10ds, large p, (2ds, p) four times, 8ds, rw.
Ring C of 6ds, join to Ring A, (6ds, p) twice, 6ds, rw.
Ring D of 8ds, join to last picot of Ring B, (2ds, p) four times, 10ds, rw.
Ring E of 6ds, join to last picot of Ring C, 6ds, rw.
Ring F of 10ds, p, (2ds, p) four times, 8ds, rw.
Ring G of 6ds, join to junction of Rings C and E, 6ds,

join to Ring C, (3ds, p) twice, 6ds, rw.
Ring H of 8ds, join to last picot of Ring F, (2ds, p) four times (making the last picot large) 10 ds, rw.
Ring I of 6ds, join to last picot of Ring G, 3ds, p, 3ds, rw.
Jk of 10hs, rw.
Ring J of 3ds, join to Ring I, 3ds, p, 6ds, rw.
Ring K as Ring B.
Ring L of 6ds, join to Ring J, 3ds, join to Ring G, 3ds, p, 6ds, p, 6ds, rw.
Complete remainder to match the opposite side. Tie a thread at the junction of Rings G and L to represent antennae.

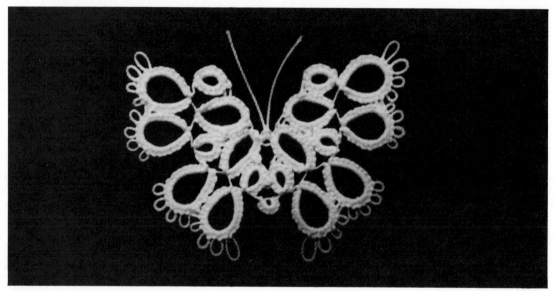

Butterfly

CROSS

Using Coats *Chain* Mercer Crochet No. 20, the cross measures 10 cm (4 in) in height.

Ring A of 6ds, p, 6ds, rw.
* Chain A of 5ds, rw.
Ring B of 12ds, p, (4ds, p) twice, 4ds, rw.
Chain B of (3ds, p) four times, 3ds, rw.
Ring C of 4ds, join to last picot of Ring B, 4ds, rw.
Chain C of (3ds, p) six times, 3ds, rw.
Ring D of 4ds, join to next picot of Ring B, 4ds, rw.
Chain D of (3ds, p) four times, 3ds, join shuttle

thread to next picot of Ring B, 5ds, rw.
Ring A of 6ds, join to previous Ring A, 6ds, rw.

Repeat from * twice more, joining successive Rings A to the centre junction.
** Chain A, Ring B, Chain B and Ring C as before.

Repeat from ** twice more.
Chain C as before.
(Ring D and Chain D) three times.
Tie to base of first Ring A to finish.

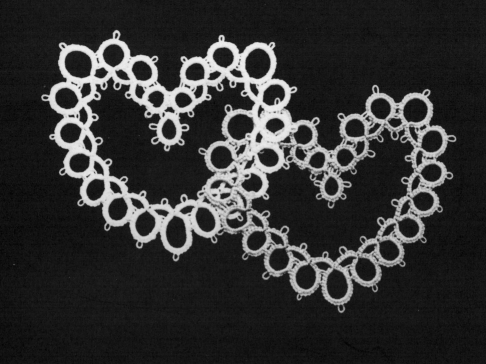

Entwined Hearts

Frog

66

Designed by Gill Fisher, these curvaceous hearts are enhanced by the use of contrasting colours. Using Coats *Chain* Mercer Crochet No. 40, each heart measures 7 cm ($2\frac{3}{4}$ in) in width, and the combined pair measure 10 cm (4 in) in width.

With approximately 50 cm (20 in) of thread on the shuttle:
Centre ring of 2ds, p, (3ds, p) six times, 1ds.
Tie and finish.

With shuttle re-wound and continuous from the ball:
Ring A of 3ds, p, 3ds, join to first picot of centre ring, (3ds, p) four times, 3ds, rw.
Chain of 3ds, p, 3ds, rw.
Ring B of 3ds, join to last picot of previous ring, 3ds, join to next picot of same ring, (6ds, p) twice, 3ds, p, 3ds, rw.
Chain as before.
Ring C of 3ds, join to last picot of previous ring, 3ds, join to next picot of same ring, (7ds, p) twice, 3ds, p, 3ds, rw.

Chain as before.
Ring D of 3ds, join to last picot of previous ring, 3ds, join to next picot of same ring, (9ds, p) twice, 3ds, p, 3ds, rw.
Chain as before.
Ring C and chain as before.
(Ring B and chain) four times. *B1 23 C*
Ring C and chain, Ring D and chain, Ring C and chain as before.
(Ring B and chain) four times.

Ring C and chain, Ring D and chain, Ring C and chain, Ring B and chain as before.
Ring A of 3ds, join to last picot of previous ring, 3ds, join to next picot of same ring, 3ds, join to corresponding picot of first Ring A, 3ds, join to next picot of same ring, 3ds, join to next picot of centre ring, 3ds, p, 3ds.
Tie ends to finish.

Make a second heart in the same way, but before working final Ring A, link the tatting through the first heart, as shown.

Using DMC *Coton Perlé* No. 5, this fastening for a pair of linked buttons measures 12 cm ($4\frac{3}{4}$ in) across, and is adaptable for any size of button. Two shuttles are needed.

First motif
Wind approximately $1\frac{1}{2}$ m ($1\frac{3}{4}$ yd) on the main shuttle and approximately $4\frac{1}{2}$ m (5 yd) on the second, so that there is a continuous thread between the shuttles.

Using main shuttle:
Large ring of 40ds—or as required for the size of the button—rw.
Chain of 3ds, small p, 1ds, rw, 3ds.

Using second shuttle:
Ring of (3ds, p) twice, (2ds, p) three times, 3ds, p, 3ds.

* Using main shuttle:
Chain of 3ds.

Using second shuttle:
Ring of 3ds, join to last picot of previous ring, 3ds, p, (2ds, p) three times, 3ds, p, 3ds.

Repeat from * four times more.

Using main shuttle:
Chain of 3ds, rw, join to small picot, 3ds.
Tie to beginning of large ring to finish.

Work a second motif to match.

67

Using Coats *Chain* Mercer Crochet No. 20, the lace measures 15 cm (6 in) in length.

Ring A of 8ds, p, 8ds, rw.
Chain A of (4ds, p) five times, 4ds, rw.
Ring B of 8ds, join to Ring A, 8ds.
Chain B of (4ds, p) three times, 4ds, rw.
Ring C of 6ds, join to last picot of Chain A (counting in the order worked), 6ds, rw.
* Chain C of (4ds, p) twice, 4ds, rw.
Ring D of 6ds, join to next picot of Chain A, 6ds, rw.
Repeat from * three times more.
Chain D of (4ds, p) three times, 4ds, join shuttle thread to base of Ring A.
Chain E of 4ds, join to last picot of Chain D, (4ds, p) three times, 4ds, rw.
Ring E of 8ds, join to junction of Rings A and B, 8ds.
Ring F of 6ds, p, 6ds, rw.
Chain F of (4ds, p) twice, 4ds, rw.
Ring G of 6ds, join to Ring F, 6ds, rw.
Chain G of 4ds, p, 4ds.
Ring H of 4ds, join to Chain G, (4ds, p) twice, 4ds.
Ring I of 4ds, join to last picot of Ring H, 4ds, p, 12ds, p, 4ds, p, 4ds.
Ring J of 4ds, join to last picot of Ring I, (4ds, p) twice, 4ds.
Chain H of 4ds, join to last picot of Ring J, 4ds, rw.
Ring K of 6ds, join to junction of Rings F and G, 6ds, rw.
Chain F as before.
Ring L of 6ds, join to junction of Rings F, G and K, 6ds.
Ring M of 8ds, join to junction of Rings A, B and E, 8ds, rw.
Chain I of (4ds, p) three times, 4ds, join to first picot of Chain B, 4ds.
Tie to base of Ring B to finish.

Work a second piece similarly, joining the two centre Chains C, as shown.
Cut ten 15 cm (6 in) lengths of thread for each tassel and attach as shown.

Gemini

JASMINE

Using Coats *Chain* Mercer Crochet No. 20, the tatting measures 5.5 cm ($2\frac{1}{4}$ in) in height, using No. 60 it measures 4 cm ($1\frac{1}{2}$ in). Two shuttles are needed, wound on a continuous thread.

First flower

Using main shuttle:

Centre ring of (4ds, small p) five times, 4ds, rw.

Chain A of 10ds, p, 2ds, join shuttle thread to last picot of centre ring.

Chain B of 2ds, join to last picot of previous chain, (4ds, p) twice, 2ds, join shuttle thread to next picot of centre ring.

Chain C as Chain B.

Chain D of 2ds, join to last picot of previous chain, 8ds, p, 2ds, join shuttle thread to next picot of centre ring.

Chain E as Chain D.

Chain F of 2ds, join to previous chain, 10ds, join shuttle thread to junction of Chain A with centre ring.

Chain G of 6ds.

Using second shuttle:

Ring of 8ds, p, 8ds.

Using main shuttle:

Chain H of 24ds.

Cut threads, leaving ends loose.

Second flower

Work centre ring and Chain A as before.

Chain B of 2ds, join to picot of previous chain, 4ds, join to Chain C of first flower as shown, 4ds, p, 2ds, join shuttle thread as before.

Chain C of 2ds, join to previous chain, 4ds, join to Chain B of first flower, 4ds, p, 2ds, join shuttle thread as before.

Complete second flower as first flower.

To finish, tie each Chain H to its opposite flower, as shown.

These intriguing forms were designed by Carol Carsten who appropriately, made her originals in mushroom-coloured thread. Using Coats *Chain* Mercer Crochet No. 20, each mushroom measures 3.5 cm ($1\frac{1}{4}$ in) in height.

Flat-topped mushroom

Using shuttle thread only:
Ring A of (3ds, p) three times, 3ds. Space of 3 mm ($\frac{1}{8}$ in).
Ring B of 5ds, join to last picot of previous ring, (5ds, p) twice, 5ds.
Space as before.
Ring C of 8ds, join to last picot of previous ring, (2ds, p) eight times, 8ds.
Space as before.
Ring D as Ring B. Space as before.
Ring E of 3ds, join to last picot of previous ring, (3ds, p) twice, 3ds, rw.

Tie ball thread to last space.

Making all joins of Chain A with the shuttle thread:
Chain A of 5ds, join to last picot of Ring E, 5ds, join to next picot of same ring, 8ds, join to next picot of Ring D, 10ds, join to centre picot of Ring C, 10ds, join to next picot of Ring B, 8ds, (join to next picot of Ring A, 5ds) twice, join to space between Rings A and B, rw.
Chain B of (5ds, p) twice, 5ds, join to last picot of same Chain B, 5ds, join to next picot of same chain, 5ds.
Tie to space between Rings D and E to finish.

Round-topped mushroom

With shuttle wound directly from ball thread:
Ring A of (3ds, p) three times, 3ds.
Ring B of 5ds, join to last picot of previous ring, (5ds, p) three times, 5ds.
Ring C of 3ds, join to last picot of previous ring, (3ds, p) twice, 3ds, rw.

Making all joints of Chain A with the shuttle thread:
Chain A of 4ds, join to last picot of Ring C, 3ds, join to next picot of same ring, (2ds, p) four times, 2ds, join to next picot of Ring B, 4ds, join to next picot of same ring, (2ds, p) four times, 2ds, join to next picot of Ring A, 3ds, join to next picot of same ring, 4ds, join to base of rings.

Chain B of 2ds, p, (3ds, p) eight times, 2ds.

Tie to base of rings to finish.

Piping cord was dyed to match the heavy ceramic beads for this necklace, which features Twisted or Spiral Tatting. Using 6 m ($6\frac{3}{4}$ yd) of fine cotton cord, the necklace measures 92 cm (36 in) in length and is adjustable. Eight matching beads are required, plus a centre bead. If a large shuttle is not available, wind the cord into a 'figure-of-eight' and secure with an elastic band.

Cut 120 cm (48 in) for the 'shuttle' cord, and slip the eight matching beads on the remaining 'ball' cord. Knot the two cords loosely together leaving ends of approximately 18 cm (7 in) in readiness for the tassel.

Chain of 20hs, slip up a bead, (2ds, bead) twice, 20hs, bead, 50ds, bead, 20hs, bead, (2ds, bead) twice, 20hs.

Untie the knot at the beginning. Knot both ends of the 'shuttle' cord together with an overhand knot, and similarly knot both ends of the 'ball' cord.
Thread the centre bead on one pair of cords, then knot all the cords together with an overhand knot.

Fray the tassel, soak it in water to straighten any kinks, and trim the ends evenly.

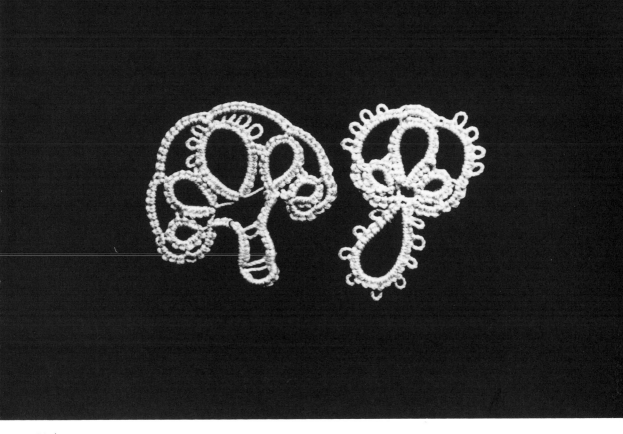

Mushrooms

Necklace

RIBBON TRIMS

Using Coats *Chain* Mercer Crochet No. 20, the tatting measures 5.5 cm ($2\frac{1}{4}$ in) across, but can be adapted for a ribbon of any width. Thread 15 small rocaille beads on the ball before starting each trim.

Ring A of (3ds, p) five times, 3ds, rw.
* Chain A of 9ds, slip up 3 beads, 9ds, rw.
Ring B of 3ds, p, 3ds, join to second picot from end of previous ring, (3ds, p) three times, 3ds, rw.
Repeat from * four times more.

Chain B of 12ds, join shuttle thread to second picot from end of previous ring, 30ds—or the number required for the width of the ribbon—join shuttle thread to corresponding picot of first Ring A, 12ds. Tie to beginning of first ring to finish.

Work a second trim similarly.

To attach the trim, enclose the long chain in a fold of ribbon and fuse with iron-on webbing.

SEAHORSE†

Using Coats *Chain* Mercer Crochet No. 20, the tatting measures 4 cm (1½ in) in height, using No. 60 it measures 2.5 cm (1 in).
Leave approximately 10 cm (4 in) of thread.
* Ring A of 6ds, p, (3ds, p) twice, 6ds.
Ring B of 6ds, join to last picot of previous ring, (3ds, p) twice, 6ds.
Work Ring B five times more, rw.
Repeat from * once more.

Cut thread, leaving an end as at the beginning.
To finish, tie the first end to centre picot of first ring of second group; tie the last end to centre picot of last ring of first group.

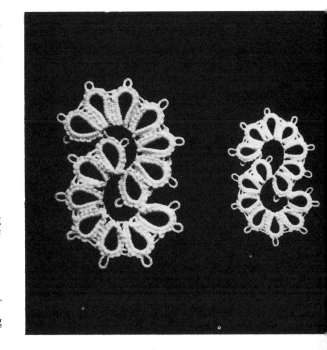

SNOWFLAKE

Using Coats *Chain* Mercer No. 40, the tatting measures 5 cm (2 in) in diameter.

Centre

Ring of 9ds, p, (4ds, p) three times, 9ds.
* Ring of 9ds, join to last picot of previous ring, (4ds, p) three times, 9ds.

Repeat from * six times more, joining last picot of last ring to first picot of first ring.
Tie threads. Take shuttle thread across back of work and join it to junction of first and last rings.

Outer round

Ring A of (3ds, p) twice, 3ds.
* Join shuttle thread to next free picot of centre.
Ring B of 3ds, join to last picot of previous ring, (2ds, p) six times, 3ds.
Join shuttle thread to next free picot of centre.
Ring C of 3ds, join to last picot of previous ring, 3ds, p, 3ds.
Join shuttle thread to next junction of centre rings.
Ring A of 3ds, join to last picot of previous ring, 3ds, p, 3ds.

Repeat from * all around, joining last Ring C to first Ring A.
Tie to junction of centre rings to finish.

Snowflake

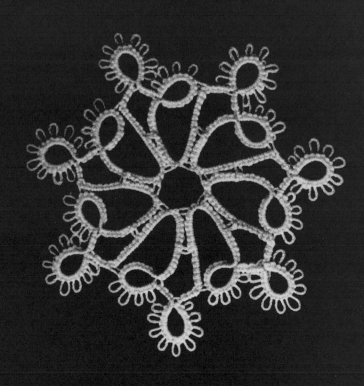

Using Coats *Chain* Mercer Crochet No. 40, the tatting measures 8 cm ($3\frac{1}{8}$ in) in diameter. Two shuttles are needed, wound on a continuous thread.

Using main shuttle:
Centre ring of (2ds, p) eleven times, 2ds. Work lock stitch to form a twelfth false picot.
Chain A of 10ds, rw.
* Ring A of 5ds, p, 5ds, rw.
Chain B of 7ds, rw.
Ring B of 7ds, p, 7ds, rw.
Chain C of 9ds.

Using second shuttle:
Ring C of (2ds, p) five times, 2ds.

Using main shuttle:
Chain D of 9ds, join main shuttle thread to Ring B, 7ds, join main shuttle thread to Ring A, small p, 10ds, join main shuttle thread to next picot of centre ring.
Chain A of 10ds, join to small picot of Chain D, 1ds, rw.
Ring A and Chain C as before.

Using second shuttle:

Ring C as before.

Using main shuttle:
Chain E of 9ds, join main shuttle thread to Ring A, small p, 10ds, join main shuttle thread to next picot of centre ring.
Chain A of 10ds, join to small picot of Chain E, 1ds, rw.

Repeat from * four times more.
Ring A, Chain B, Ring B and Chain C as before.

Using second shuttle:
Ring C as before.

Using main shuttle:
Chain D, Chain A, Ring A and Chain C as before.

Using second shuttle:
Ring C as before.

Using main shuttle:
Chain E of 9ds, join main shuttle thread to previous Ring A, join second shuttle thread to base of first Ring A, 10ds.

Tie to false picot of centre ring to finish.

Using Coats *Chain* Mercer Crochet No. 40, the tatting measures 6 cm ($2\frac{3}{8}$ in) in diameter.

Ring A of (2ds, p) nine times, 2ds, rw.
Chain A of 3ds, rw.
Ring B of (2ds, p) five times, 10ds, rw.
Chain B of (7ds, p) twice, 2ds, p, 7ds, p, 7ds, join shuttle thread to last picot of Ring B, 3ds, rw.
* Ring A, Chain A and Ring B as before.
Chain B of 7ds, join to last picot of previous Chain B, 7ds, join to next picot of same chain, 2ds, p, 7ds, p, 7ds, join shuttle thread to last picot of previous Ring B, 3ds, rw.
Repeat from * four times more.
Ring A, Chain A and Ring B as before.
Chain B of 7ds, join to last picot of previous Chain B, 7ds, join to next picot of same chain, 2ds, join to corresponding picot of first Chain B, 7ds, join to next picot of same chain, 7ds, join shuttle thread to Ring B, 3ds.

Tie to base of first Ring A to finish.

TRIAD

Using Coats *Chain* Mercer Crochet No. 20, the tatting measures 6.5 cm (2½ in) in width. Two shuttles are needed, wound on a continuous thread.

Using main shuttle:
Ring A of 6ds, p, 6ds, rw.
Chain A of 6ds, p, 6ds, p, 10ds, rw.
Ring B of 6ds, join to Ring A, 6ds, rw.
Chain B of 6ds, p, 3ds.

Using second shuttle:
Jk of 8hs.

Using main shuttle:
Continue Chain B with 3ds, rw.
Ring C of 6ds, join to junction of rings, 6ds.
Chain C of (6ds, p) four times, 6ds.
Ring D of 6ds, p, 6ds, rw.
Chain D of 3ds.

Using second shuttle:
Jk of 8hs.

Using main shuttle:

Continue Chain D with 3ds, join to corresponding picot of Chain B, 6ds, rw.
Ring A of 6ds, join to Ring D, 6ds, rw.
Chain E of 10ds, join to corresponding picot of Chain A, 2ds, p, 10ds, rw.
Ring B of 6ds, join to junction of rings, 6ds, rw.
Chain B and Ring C as before.
Chain F of (6ds, p) twice, 3ds.

Using second shuttle:
Ring E of (3ds, p) three times, 3ds.

Using main shuttle:
Continue Chain F with 3ds, p, 6ds, p, 6ds.
Ring D, Chain D and Ring A as before.
Chain E of 10ds, join to corresponding picot of previous Chain E, 2ds, p, 10ds, rw.
Ring B, Chain B, Ring C, Chain C, Ring D, Chain D and Ring A as before.
Chain G of 10ds, join to corresponding picot of previous Chain E, 6ds, p, 6ds, rw.
Ring B as before.

Tie ends to finish.

76

FURTHER READING

More patterns can be found in the following publications. Information on basic techniques can be found in the books marked * and information on Roll Tatting and Pearl Tatting can be found in those marked **.

Anne Orr's Classic Tatting Patterns, Dover Publications, 1985

Attenborough, Bessie M., *The Craft of Tatting,* * Bell & Hyman, 1985

Jones, Rebecca, *The Complete Book of Tatting,* * ** Dryad Press/Kangaroo Press, 1985

Konior, Mary, *A Pattern Book of Tatting,* * Dryad Press, 1985

Konior Mary, *Tatting in Lace,* * ** Dryad Press, 1988

Sanders, Julia E., *Tatting Patterns,* Dover Publications, 1977

Weiss, Rita, *Tatting Doilies and Edgings,* Dover Publications, 1980

Weiss, Rita, *Traditional Tatting Patterns,* Dover Publications, 1986

York, Sheila, *Projects in Tatting,* * Dryad Press, 1985

SUPPLIERS

Shuttles, threads and accessories are available by mail order from:

D. J. Hornsby,
149 High Street,
Burton Latimer,
Kettering,
Northants,
NN15 5RL

A. Sells,
49 Pedley Lane,
Clifton,
Shefford,
Bedfordshire

Sebalace,
Waterloo Mill,
Howden Road,
Silsden,
West Yorkshire,
BD20 0AH

Lindalace,
Value House,
12 Union Road,
Croydon,
Surrey,
CRO 2XU

Galleon Crafts,
72 Church Street,
Whitby,
North Yorkshire

Lacis,
2982 Adeline Street,
Berkeley,
California 94703,
USA

Needlework,
Bucklers Farm,
Coggeshall,
Essex,
CO6 1SB

Frivolité,
15526 Densmore N.,
Seattle,
Washington 98133,
USA

Craftsman-made shuttles:

silver from

Rattenburys,
127 Hereson Road,
Ramsgate,
Kent,
CT11 7EE

wood, inlaid or
painted, from

D. and C. Springett,
21 Hillmorton Road,
Rugby,
Warwickshire,
CV22 5DF

wood, painted, from

Ann Keller,
Coolvally,
Abingdon Park,
Shankill,
Co. Dublin,
Ireland

wood, polished, from

A. P. Kingston,
'Erw-Las',
Llanddewi,
Llandrindod Wells,
Powys,
LD1 6SE

wood, flat notched model,
from

Jack Bamsey,
12 Fir Close,
West Moors,
Wimborne,
Dorset,
BH22 0LF

Tunbridge Ware from

Peter Benjamin,
11 London Road,
Tonbridge,
Kent,
TN10 3AB

silver, ivory, horn, shell
and other materials from

Lacis, (address above)

Large shuttles, 4 to 6 inches in length, also from
Lacis

Further information from:

The British College of Lace,
21 Hillmorton Road,
Rugby,
Warwickshire,
CV22 5DF

The English Lace School,
Oak House,
Church Stile,
Woodbury,
Devon
EX5 1HP

The Lace Guild,
The Hollies,
53 Audnam,
Stourbridge,
West Midlands,
DY8 4AE

Nineteenth-century parasol cover in tatting, The English Lace School

INDEX